Noise Pollution

Noise Pollution

Donald F. Anthrop
San Jose State University

Lexington Books
D.C. Heath and Company
Lexington, Massachusetts
Toronto   London

Library of Congress Cataloging in Publication Data

Anthrop, Donald F.
    1. Noise pollution. I. Title.
TD892.A57   620.2'3   73-6615
ISBN 0-669-85662-2

Published simultaneously in Canada.

Printed in the United States of America.

International Standard Book Number: 0-669-85662-2

Library of Congress Catalog Card Number: 73-994

Contents

List of Figures

List of Tables

Foreword

"Cotton Wool for Your Ears," it says on a little envelope available to BOAC's trans-Atlantic passengers. A strange but pleasant and innocuous gift, I thought, but who needs it? The inside of the VC-10 was quiet enough and so was the inside of a Boeing 707 on which I found my second envelope. There was no reason thus to insulate myself from reality within the craft. I still keep the envelopes, however, for the day I shall be testifying against supersonic transports, or other aural assaults on people and places. I intend to use the BOAC gift as an exhibit in favor of quiet.

"If cotton is to be put in ears," the testimony could argue, "let it not be wasted on the passengers whose travel habits support the noise. Give it to the millions of innocents who must suffer in nonsilence for the convenience of the high-flown speeders.

"If these millions must be made to suffer further," I could go on, "by finding themselves, through no fault of their own, on a sonic-boom carpet—the wall-to-wall covering which the ultimate SST flight patterns would lay upon the globe—then why not provide them with something far more adequate than a tiny wad of cotton? Why not an early warning service, financed by the airlines and their fast travelers, that would let everyone on the carpet know of each threat of sonic bang in time to prepare for it? Provide stereo headsets for all, and compact tape players, with adequate amplification, to produce beautiful music or pleasant natural sounds with enough volume within the headset to overpower the ugly booms."

Few who believe that the market economy can put a proper price on everything will be willing to go this far in setting the price for an SST ticket. But we should consider going much farther still.

Since the sonic boom would be only part of the insult wished upon the millions by the SST-hooked few, we should weigh several other requirements of equity. The Internal Revenue Code ought to be amended to provide fast and sure compensation for the sufferers. Taxpayers who believed themselves damaged by SSTs could withhold from their withholding tax their best estimate of what the damage amounted to; it would be up to the government to prove them wrong and supply them counsel at no charge to help them contend with the government. Damage could be awarded to cover not only what the booms would inflict on property, pets, loved ones, wildlife, and wilderness, but also for the per-person allocation of damage done to the ozone barrier. There could be a further withholding to offset reasonably predicted prospective damage. For example, fuel and travel costs would double or treble for people willing to travel no faster than ten miles per minute. This would result from the unconscionable fuel-gulping SSTs require to achieve extra noise and speed for jet-set convenience. Operation of a fleet of 500 Boeing SSTs, recently advocated by the

Administration, would require the discovery of five more Prudhoe Bays by the year 2,000—*just for the surplus speed.* This extirpation of oil would probably raise the ordinary man's fuel costs far more than by a factor of three. If so, withhold more from taxes.

A major benefit of thus assessing the true cost of a technological nonnecessity becomes clear: collection of income taxes would cease and the government would owe money to all its citizens, the cost of this revolutionary improvement in the financial state of the world's slow-moving citizens being borne wholly by SST travelers.

This proposal is of course too logical to be countenanced. Far better to require the tortoise-minded many to become inured to stresses that benefit the harebrained few. Clearly, putting fair compensation into proper time frame and programming it as a computer input would be too hard.

The example, I'll admit, seems far-fetched. Let us look at a near-fetched one. How could one calculate who owed whom how much for the following noisy inconvenience: At George Washington's headquarters for the Battle of Yorktown there recently assembled a crew of television producers, directors, scriptwriters, cameramen, soundmen, assistants, and alleged star to produce a one-minute commercial that alluded to the earth's wild places. To get that one minute required seven hours. The sounds of battle had left long before, but there were new sounds. Some were surprises—a slamming car door as a tourist moved in to watch, or a gunning motor as he left. Others could be foreseen (or foreheard, perhaps)—oncoming planes, small and large, low and high, prop and jet, seen through the springtime lacery of branches filled with birdsong, headed inexorably toward General Washington's command post and into the sound track. The extra six hours of production time was expensive, but how, once you had priced it out, would you ever know where to send the bills?

Leave the accounting to the government, then, and withhold the cost to you from your income tax! The government should either protect the people from disturbances of the people's peace with unsound noise, or the government should desist from charging citizens for nonservice given.

Call the whole proposal facetious, but keep it in mind. Remember it as you recall all the beautiful sounds that used to be your inalienable right from the time you arrived on the planet for your brief pass at it. Remember it as you take inventory of the various kinds of din that lately have been drowning out your right, not by your leave, and without due process of law and with no compensation at all. Think of the loss as property stolen from you, one of the nicest things you used to own, your chance for serenity on call.

Remembering such things, we can be grateful for what Don Anthrop has done in a very practical way to identify the thieves who noisily steal away silence. He gives us ways to measure what they have taken from us already and are planning to take more of as fast and loudly as they can. He shows us example after example of how some imaginative people in various parts of the United States and elsewhere about the planet have gone about stopping the thieves at the threshold.

Professor Anthrop has assembled for us here, in descriptive text, illustration, and documentation, an array of weapons with which we may peacefully defend ourselves. With his help we will hear the world's music again, and the cacophony that obscured it will be reduced to decent limits.

A decent limit ought to include freedom from sonic booms not only on the land, but also over the sea, where the great whales, we should concede, have precedence on the principal travel routes. The whales could then continue their own communication across the wide oceans, with a little silence preserved for them through our own exercise of reasonable restraint. They knew a certain silence when they went back to sea sixty-five million years ago; in a mere century man has already found too many ways to disrupt it. Being this considerate about whales could serve our own self-interest: a world in which the whales find their quiet will be a pleasanter one for people than ours has become lately.

We should like to see continuing editions of this work, encompassing what many of us will have accomplished because the tools are here at hand.

David R. Brower, *President*
Friends of the Earth

1 The Situation

The same factors which have brought us air and water pollution in crisis proportions, namely increasing population, urbanization, industrialization, technological change, and the usual relegation of environmental considerations to a position of secondary importance relative to economic ones, have also brought us a crescendo of noise.

Environmental noise pollution is not an entirely new phenomenon, but rather is a problem that has grown steadily worse with time. A poem written about 1350 complains about the noise made by blacksmiths, and early references to street noises in London date back to the early 1800s. Even in eighteenth century Philadelphia, Ben Franklin felt compelled to move from High Street to Second and Sassafras because "the din of the Market increases upon me; and that, with frequent interruptions, has, I find, made me say some things twice over."[1] In the intervening years, the noise nuisance has escalated dramatically in both its severity and extent. As Art Seidenbaum remarked, in his column in the Los Angeles *Times* in 1967, "The day of the decibels is upon us and aural air pollution has become one of the issues of survival."[2]

Prolonged exposure to intense noise produces permanent hearing loss. Very much lower noise levels, however, interfere with normal conversation, hinder concentrated mental effort, induce stress, cause inefficiency at work, prevent sleep, cause irritability, and interfere with relaxation and recreation. Fatigue and inadequate rest caused by a noisy home environment coupled with distraction and impaired mental concentration of employees while on the job result in incalculable economic losses to employers. Unfortunately, people suffering from stress and emotional disturbances frequently do not realize that noise may be an important contributing factor. Furthermore, aside from considerations of health and human productivity, like polluted streams, smoke-filled air, and ugliness of slums, noise degrades the quality of our lives and detracts from the enjoyment of urban living.

While the population explosion and social and economic changes have contributed to the increasing noise levels in the community, technological change must bear the greatest responsibility. Dr. Leo Beranek, a world-renowned acoustics expert, recently remarked, "Modern technology has furnished its own fanfare—an ever-increasing din that disturbs our sleep, interrupts our conversation, creates anxiety and annoyance, and sometimes damages hearing."[3]

The products of this technology have, to be sure, released mankind from some of the more immediate problems of survival. But, for far too long, noise has been regarded as a necessary price of technological "progress." Indeed, Professor Gunther Lehman, president of the International Association Against Noise has observed, "Noise is not a measure of the progress of technology, but a sign of regression."[4]

Yet the view held by some that technology per se is responsible for all of our environmental ills is an oversimplification of the matter, as is the converse notion that technology is a universal solvent that, having liberated Western man from the bondage of poverty and disease, need only be applied more vigorously to assure global prosperity and universal happiness. In its report, *Technology: Process of Assessment and Choice*, the U.S. National Academy of Science has observed:

Between these two extremes lies the view of those who recognize that benefit and injury alike may flow from technology, which after all, is nothing more than a systematic way of altering the environment. . . The choice, from this perspective, is not between the abandonment of technology as a tool of human aspirations and the uncontrolled pursuit of technology as though more tools invariably meant a better life. The choice, rather is between technological advance that proceeds without adequate consideration of its consequences and technological change that is influenced by a deeper concern for the interactions between man's tools and the human environment in which they do their work.[5]

While noise is primarily an urban problem, the noisy machines that man insists on building are increasingly bringing noise pollution to the few remaining wild places in the world. Escape from manmade sound is infinitely more difficult today than in Ben Franklin's time, and within another half-century it may be impossible. A few examples will illustrate the extent of this problem. The California desert, extending from the Sierra Nevada and Death Valley southward some 240 miles to the Mexican border, and from the Colorado River westward over 100 miles to the San Bernardino Mountains bordering Los Angeles, comprises more than 16 million acres of public land. Yet on any weekend during the winter months, one has difficulty escaping the roar of dune buggies and motorcycles that are being used off maintained roads (and which, incidentally, are doing irreparable damage to the fragile desert ecology), the whine of commercial jet aircraft in the flight pattern for Los Angeles International Airport, and sonic booms produced by military aircraft. The stony silence of the Brooks range in Alaska is now shattered by aircraft transporting people and supplies between Fairbanks and the oilfields on the north slope. Increasingly, the solitude of remote areas of both Canada and Alaska is being broken by light aircraft in the summer and by the incredibly noisy snowmobile during the winter. Alaska Airlines, eager to build a booming tourist business, has built a hotel in Nome and now flies its Boeing 727 jets into this tiny town on the Bering Sea.

Between 1968 and 1970 jet noise was introduced to a number of remote places in the Canadian arctic. By the end of 1971 Nordair had four Boeing 737 aircraft which were in service on routes between Montreal and Great Whale, Fort Chimo, Frobisher Bay, and Resolute Bay. Pacific Western had four Boeing 737s in its fleet, some of which were in service on routes between Edmonton, Alberta, and Fort Smith, Hay River, Yellowknife, Norman Wells, Inuvik, Cambridge Bay, and Resolute (all in N.W.T.), while Quebecair was operating BAC-111 aircraft between Montreal and Churchill Falls, Nfd. In addition, of course, some of these areas were already traversed by intercontinental air traffic. If airlines are permitted to fly supersonic transports, the sound of man's technology may be inflicted upon nearly every square mile of land on this planet by the turn of the century.

One might well ask how we managed to arrive at the present state of affairs. Several contributing factors would seem to be responsible. Perhaps most important has been the consistent capitulation to technology and gross national product by public officials at all levels of government. Secondly, noise, unlike air and water pollution, cannot be visually determined and leaves no visible record of its presence. Finally, noise is inherently a technical problem which the ordinary citizen has great difficulty understanding. While he doesn't understand the complex chemistry of air pollution, he can nevertheless *see* that the air is polluted and demand remedial action by government. Because of the technical nature of noise and because scientific instruments are needed for its measurement, the ordinary citizen has great difficulty in organizing a strong protest against the aural assault to which he is subjected. If he does protest, he must rely almost exclusively on subjective values which cannot readily be translated into physical criteria or legislation and which are ·vulnerable to attack by special interests armed with scientific measurements.

While the abatement of much of the noise that presently plagues industrialized societies is in part a technical problem, science alone will not provide answers. Solutions carry price tags, and although our scientific capability must be improved, in this as in all situations where the quality of life for people in a democratic society is in conflict with various economic interests, the balance is struck in the political arena. Lawmaking, then, is of paramount importance in the control of environmental noise.

However, existing legal remedies have proved to be inadequate. In the first place, nuisance suits have met with very limited success. Secondly, recovery of monetary damages from a noise maker has been difficult at best for the ordinary citizen and, even when successful, does not constitute any real solution to the problem of environmental noise. Finally, many existing laws and ordinances enacted for the purpose of controlling environmental noise have proved unenforceable because they either have failed to spell out in quantitative terms noise levels at which violations would occur or have failed to provide suitable methods for measuring such noise levels. For these reasons, an understanding of the physical concepts of noise and its measurement is essential for effective legislation in the field.

2

Sound as Noise

Acoustical Terminology

What is noise? Noise is usually defined as unwanted sound, and sound is the result of the transfer of mechanical vibration to air. Thus problems of sound and vibration are intimately related. Just as mechanical vibration can produce sound, extremely intense sounds, such as those made by low-flying jet aircraft, can produce mechanical vibration and even structural damage.

Whenever an object vibrates, it disturbs the air molecules near the object and sets them in vibration also. These molecular vibrations produce small variations of definite frequency and amplitude in the normal atmospheric air pressure (see Figure 2-1). *Amplitude* is a measure of the magnitude of these pressure variations. Anything that vibrates has a frequency of vibration. *Frequency* is the number of vibrations per second that occur, and it is usually expressed in *cycles per second*, or *hertz* (abbreviated Hz), which are synonymous. In the case of sound, frequency determines the *pitch* of the sound. Low frequency sounds have a low pitch; high frequency sounds have a high pitch. The lowest note on the piano has a frequency of 27 Hz and the highest note has a frequency of 4,186 Hz. The disturbance spreads outward from the source and when the pressure variations reach our eardrums they are translated by our hearing mechanism into the sensation we call sound. The amplitude of these pressure variations is extremely small in relation to the normal atmospheric air pressure. The pressure amplitudes of the loudest sounds which the human ear can tolerate are less than 0.03 percent of the normal atmospheric air pressure. Pressure amplitude and its relation to the normal atmospheric air pressure are illustrated in Figure 2-1. These pressure variations can also be detected and measured with a sound pressure level meter without the presence of a human observer.

The pressure amplitude is a measure of sound *intensity*, that is, the rate at which sound energy is transmitted by the sound wave to a surface, per square centimeter of surface area. If P is the root-mean-square pressure amplitude of the sound, expressed in dynes per square centimeter, the intensity I in watts per square centimeter, is given by the relation

$$I = 2.37 \times 10^{-9} P^2 \qquad (1)$$

for air at standard conditions (20°C., 760 mm Hg). The human ear is a truly remarkable organ. It can discern sounds whose intensities are but 1×10^{16}

5

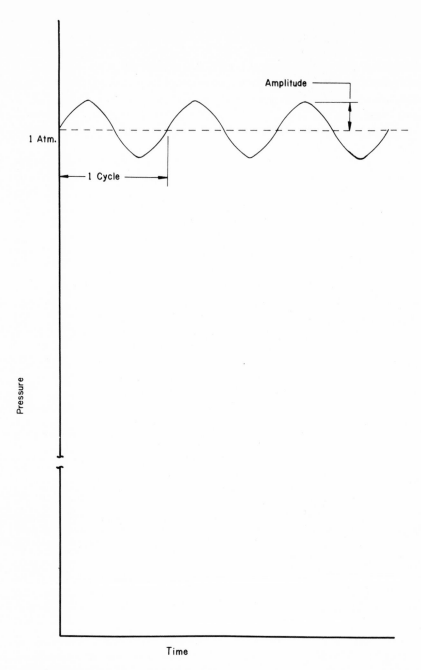

Figure 2-1. Relationship of Pressure Amplitude and Frequency of a Sound Wave to Normal Atmospheric Air Pressure.

watts per square centimeter, and it responds without damage to sounds one trillion times as intense. In contrast, the human eye responds to a light intensity range of only 100,000.

Compared with usual electrical power, the amount of power produced by sound generators is usually quite small. The average sound power developed by a person speaking in a normal conversational tone is about 10^{-5} watts. If all 21 million inhabitants of Canada were to speak at the same time, the total acoustic power developed would be approximately 200 watts or enough power to operate a fairly large light bulb.

Because of the very large range of intensities over which the human ear responds, use of a linear scale for the expression of acoustic intensities would be very difficult. If, for example, we were to measure the noise levels in a suburban residential area at night and on a street corner in any large city during the daytime, we would find the sound intensity at the city location to be about 10,000 times greater than the intensity in the suburban location. If, now, we were to attempt to plot our results on a piece of graph paper using a linear scale, we would need a very long piece of graph paper indeed. Because of this difficulty, a logarithmic rather than a linear scale is used for the expression of sound intensities. The unit is the *decibel* (abbreviated dB) and the *intensity level*, or sound level, is given by 10 times the logarithm of the ratio of the sound intensity to the intensity at the threshold of audible sound, namely 10^{-16} watts/cm^2. Put in mathematical form this relation becomes

$$IL = 10 \log \frac{I}{10^{-16}} = 10 \log I + 160 \tag{2}$$

where I is the intensity and IL is the intensity level or sound level, expressed in decibels. On the decibel scale, the sound level just detectable by the young adult with good hearing (that is, the threshold intensity of 10^{-16} watts/cm^2) is given a value of zero decibels. Because of the logarithmic nature of the decibel scale, a sound whose intensity is 10^{-15} watts/cm^2 is 10 times as intense as this threshold and its intensity level is 10 dB; a sound whose intensity is 10^{-14} watts/cm^2 is 100 times as intense as the threshold and its intensity level is 20 dB. A sound level of 50 dB is 10 times as intense as one of 40 dB and 100,000 times as intense as the threshold. The relation between intensity and the decibel scale is shown in Figure 2-2. However, the 50 dB sound is not 10 times as *loud* as the one of 40 dB. If we listen to a sound whose *intensity* is gradually increased, the sensation we call *loudness* increases also, but loudness is by no means proportional to intensity. Rather, the sensation of loudness has been found to double with approximately each 10 dB increase in intensity level. Therefore, the 50 dB sound is twice as loud as one of 40 dB and four times as loud as one of 30 dB.

While the logarithmic decibel scale keeps the numbers to a manageable level, some problems arise when one tries to add the sound levels from two different

SOUND INTENSITY	DECIBELS	
(Multiple of threshold intensity)		
1,000,000,000,000	120	Threshold of pain
100,000,000,000	110	
10,000,000,000	100	
1,000,000,000	90	
100,000,000	80	
10,000,000	70	
1,000,000	60	
100,000	50	
10,000	40	
1,000	30	
100	20	
10	10	
1	0	Threshold of hearing

Figure 2-2. Relation Between Sound Intensity, Shown as Multiples of the Intensity at the Threshold of Hearing, and the Logarithmic Decibel Scale.

sources. Consider, for example, two motorcycles each producing 90 dB. Since the total sound power emitted by the two vehicles is twice that for a single motorcycle, the total sound intensity at any given distance from the two motorcycles will also be twice that for only one. From Figure 2-2, it is obvious, however, that a doubling of the intensity does not result in a doubling of the decibel level. In order to calculate the sound level produced by the two vehicles, we use Equation (2). Substituting 90 dB into that equation, we find that the sound intensity for one motorcycle is 10^{-7} watts/cm^2. Since the total sound intensity for two motorcycles is twice that for only one, substitution of 2×10^{-7} watts/cm^2 for I in Equation (2) yields 93 dB for the sound level generated by the two vehicles. Regardless of the level, doubling the intensity of a sound results in a 3 dB increase in the sound level. This concept has two important applications. Suppose, first of all, that one sound source is producing an 80 dB level at a given location while another source is producing a 75 dB level at the same location. From Equation (2) we can readily calculate that the combined sound level from the two sources at the point in question is 81.2 dB. Therefore, elimination of the 75 dB sound source would result in only a 1.2 dB decrease (from 81.2 to 80) in the sound level at the point in question, while elimination of the 80 dB source would achieve a 6.2 dB reduction in the overall level. Secondly, in the measurement of environmental noise we frequently face the problem of trying to measure the noise level of a particular source in the presence of ambient or "background" noise. Suppose that we are attempting to measure the noise level of a motor vehicle in a location where the ambient noise level is 80 dB. Suppose that we find the total noise level with the motor vehicle operating is 90 dB. Using Equation (2) to calculate the intensities of the total noise and the ambient noise, subtracting the ambient noise intensity from the total, and substituting the resultant intensity into Equation (2), we find that the sound level produced by the motor vehicle is 89.5 dB. From this example we see that unless the level of ambient noise is at least 10 dB below the level of the source being investigated, a correction should be applied for the ambient noise.

We know that the farther we remove ourselves from an intense noise source, the less audible becomes the sound. Clearly, a jet aircraft passing overhead at 300 feet produces a much higher sound level than it would at 3,000 feet. In order to understand the relation between sound intensity and distance from the source, let us consider Figure 2-3. Suppose that the point source shown in the figure is in the air far removed from any other objects, including the ground, and is radiating sound uniformly in all directions. Let us enclose this source in an imaginary sphere of radius r. The area of this sphere is given by the well-known formula $4\pi r^2$. Let us now enclose the source in a larger sphere of radius $2r$. The area of this larger sphere is $4\pi(2r)^2 = 16\pi r^2$, or four times the area of the smaller one. Since the same amount of sound energy is now reaching a surface four times as large as before, the sound intensity at the surface will be only 1/4 of the intensity at the surface of the smaller sphere. Thus we see that increasing the distance between the source and the surface of the sphere by a factor of 2 results in a decrease in sound intensity of $(2)^2$ or 4. In summary we can say that *doubling the distance between the source and the listener results in a 6 dB decrease in sound level.* In real life, sound sources rarely behave as point sources in a free field, either because the characteristics of the source are such that the sound is not radiated uniformly in all directions or because reflecting surfaces are present. Even if the source does not radiate uniformly in all directions, the sound level still decreases 6 dB with each doubling of the distance from the source provided that the distance from the source to the measuring point is at least several times the largest dimension of the source and provided that the source is well removed from other objects. To a reasonable approximation then, a motorcycle producing a 92 dB noise level at 50 feet would create an 86 dB level at 100 feet.

We saw earlier that mechanical vibrations, and hence also sound waves, have associated with them both an amplitude and a frequency. The young adult with good hearing can discern sounds which have frequencies between about 20 and 20,000 Hz. However, the human ear is by no means equally sensitive across this entire frequency range. The ear's greatest sensitivity occurs at a frequency of about 1,000 Hz and decreases at both higher and lower frequencies. The result is that while the loudness sensation approximately doubles with each 10 dB increase in intensity level for sounds whose frequencies are close to 1,000 Hz,

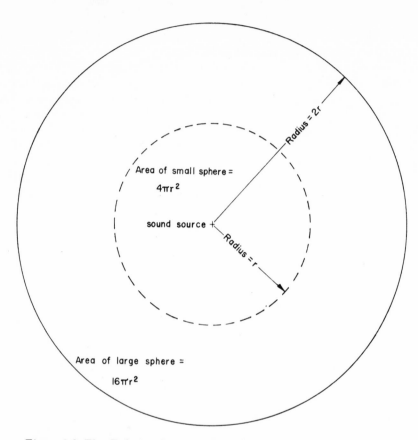

Figure 2-3. The Relation Between Sound Intensity and Distance from the Source. Note: The inner sphere of radius r has an area of $4\pi r^2$, while the larger sphere has twice the radius and four times the surface area. Consequently, the sound intensity at the surface of the larger sphere is one-fourth that at the surface of the smaller one.

this relationship does not hold true across the entire frequency range of audible sound. Many psychoacoustical experiments have been done in which listeners are asked to rate the loudness of various sounds. One approach has been to determine the intensity levels of pure tones of various frequencies that sound just as loud to a listener as a 1,000 Hz tone of some given intensity level. Such a series of measurements yields equal loudness contours. In Figure 2-4 contours of equal loudness have been plotted on a graph of the auditory area of a person with good hearing. The number on each curve is the sound level of the 1,000 Hz tone used for comparison for that curve. For example, from the 60 dB contour we see that a sound level of 60 dB at 1,000 Hz is equally as loud as one of 70 dB

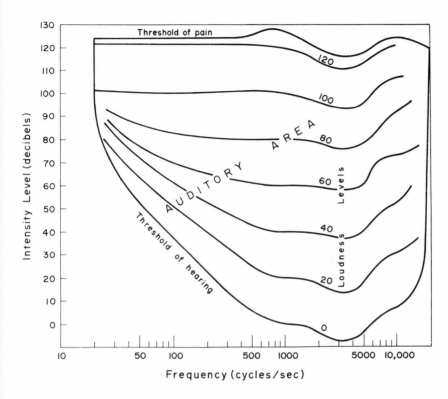

Figure 2-4. Auditory Area of a Person with Good Hearing. Note: Equal loudness contours are shown plotted against intensity level and frequency. The bottom curve, for zero loudness, is the threshold of hearing, while the top curve represents the threshold of pain.

at 100 Hz. The bottom curve for zero loudness is the threshold of hearing and represents the intensity level of the faintest sound of that frequency which can be heard. Several investigators have devised various scales for rating the loudness of noises. While these efforts have met with some success in scaling certain kinds of noises, because of the characteristics of the human ear outlined above, comparison of noises with greatly differing or complex frequencies is difficult, and no satisfactory means of rating the psychological annoyance of different kinds of noises has yet been devised.

The most commonly used instrument for the measurement of noise is the sound level meter. Most such instruments have been designed with electronic "weighting" networks which selectively discriminate against high and low frequencies. The most widely used of these weighting networks is the so-called A-weighted scale which has a response that corresponds reasonably well with that of the human ear. When this weighting network is used, the measurements are expressed in decibels on the A-weighted scale [abbreviated dB(A)]. Intensity levels, expressed in dB(A), for a number of familiar sounds are shown in Figure 2-5. The A-weighted scale is widely used for measuring noise levels outdoors, such as in traffic noise surveys and surveys of noise in the community. Most such instruments also have a "flat" scale which has an essentially uniform response over the frequency range 25 to about 20,000 Hz. Since the various weighting networks in effect discard part of the sound energy in the lower frequency ranges, one usually obtains considerably different readings depending upon whether a weighting network, such as the A-scale, is used or whether the frequency response is "flat" or uniform. For this reason, when measurements are taken with a sound level meter using one of the weighting networks, the scale should always be specified [for example, dB(A)]. When the "flat" scale is used, the results are usually reported simply as dB.

While the sound level meter is an extremely useful instrument for the measurement of many noises, such measurements do not indicate how the sound energy is distributed over the frequency spectrum. Since people react differently to a high-frequency squeal than to a low-frequency roar, a more detailed analysis of the composition of noise as a function of frequency is sometimes necessary. The most commonly used instrument for such a frequency analysis is an octave band analyzer. In such an analysis, the acoustical energy is electronically separated into various frequency bands, such as octave bands. An octave is any frequency range in which the upper frequency response is twice the lower frequency. Prior to 1960 a series of octave bands with the following frequency ranges were widely used: 75 to 150, 150 to 300, 300 to 600, 600 to 1,200, 1,200 to 2,400, 2,400 to 4,800, and 4,800 to 9,600 Hz. The preferred series of octave bands in use today consists of ten bands whose center frequencies instead of the frequency ranges are specified. The center frequencies of these bands are 31.5, 63, 125, 250, 500, 1,000, 2,000, 4,000, 8,000, and 16,000 Hz. The center frequency of an octave band is not the arithmetic mean of the high and low cutoff frequencies, but rather their geometric mean. The geometric mean is equal to $\sqrt{f_L \cdot f_H}$ where f_L and f_H are the low and high frequency band cutoffs respectively. Since $f_H = 2f_L$, the geometric mean, or the center frequency, is equal to $\sqrt{2} f_L$.

For a still more detailed analysis of the frequency distribution of sound energy even narrower bands are used. The next most widely used instrument is a one-third octave band analyzer which simply divides each octave into three one-third octaves. Instruments with still narrower band widths are available. A detailed discussion of frequency analysis is beyond the scope of this work, and the reader who desires more information on this subject should consult one of the excellent reference works listed in the references for this chapter.[1,2,3,4] Two points should be emphasized here, however. One is, that if we have one-third octave band data, we could calculate octave band data. However, one

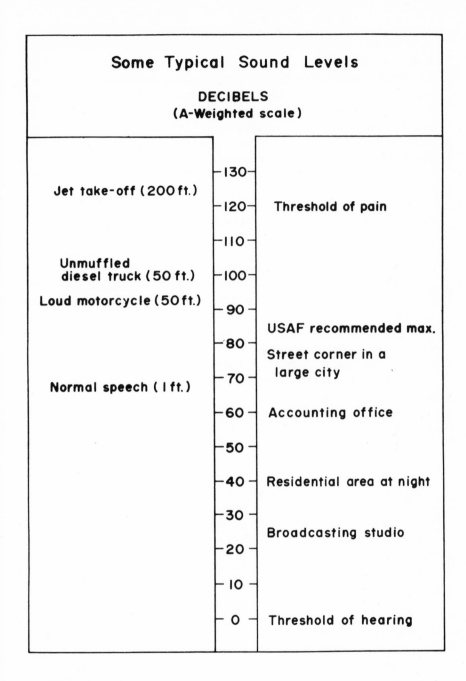

Figure 2-5. Intensity Levels, Measured in dB(A), for a Number of Familiar Sounds.

14

cannot calculate one-third octave band data from an octave band analysis. Similarly, from octave band data we could calculate overall intensity levels or A-weighted sound levels, but one cannot calculate octave band data from an overall intensity level measurement made with a sound level meter. The second point is that as one divides the frequency spectrum into smaller and smaller bands, the sound energy in any one band decreases and hence the measured sound level of each band also decreases. In the case of one-third octave band analyses, the sound energy in three one-third octave bands equals that in the corresponding full octave band. Clearly, therefore, the sound level in each of the octave bands will be less than an overall sound level measured with a sound level meter.

Effects on Man—Physiological and Psychological

A diagrammatic view of the ear is presented in Figure 2-6. The pressure variations associated with the passage of a sound wave are focused on the tympanic membrane from the outer ear canal. Three extremely tiny bones, called the middle ear ossicles, transmit the sound energy to the fluid-filled inner ear or cochlea. A diagram of the cochlea is shown in Figure 2-7. Transformation of hydraulic pressure variations within the fluid-filled cochlea into neural impulses that can be transmitted to the brain is accomplished within the Organ of Corti. This transformation is accomplished at the tiny hair cells which are in contact with the tectorial membrane. In this respect, the Organ of Corti performs a function analogous to that of the retina of the eye.

When young persons with good hearing are tested, a curve similar to the

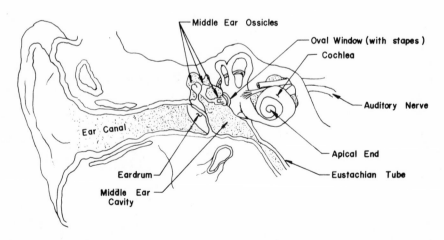

Figure 2-6. Diagrammatic View of the Human Ear.

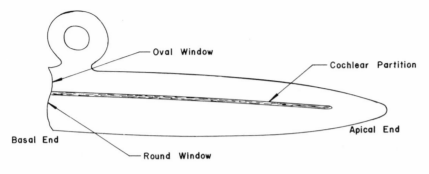

Figure 2-7. Longitudinal Cross-Section of the Unrolled Cochlea.

bottom curve in Figure 2-4 is determined. This is called a threshold curve and shows the level of the faintest sound that can just be heard by the listener. The threshold curve shows that at low frequencies, the sound intensity must be relatively high before the sound can be heard. However, in the frequency range 500 to 10,000 Hz we can hear sounds even though the intensity is very low.

Exposure to intense noise may lead to a hearing loss, which will appear as a shift in the hearing threshold. Some of the hearing loss which results from exposure to intense noise is usually temporary, and over a period of time, possibly as long as several weeks, partial or complete recovery will occur. Such temporary loss is usually referred to as temporary threshold shift (TTS). Any hearing loss which persists is called permanent threshold shift or noise induced permanent threshold shift (NIPTS). Permanent threshold shift is associated with the destruction of the hair cells in the cochlea. Hence, once a permanent threshold shift has occurred, normal hearing cannot be restored.

In some recent work, Göran Bredberg performed postmortem examinations on 119 cochleas of 74 patients. He found that the most hair cells were present in the fetal cochleas and that there was a progressive loss of hair cells from birth on. At age twenty years, about 90 percent of the hair cells remained, and at thirty years, approximately 85 percent of the cells remained. Furthermore, the exact percentage varied with the location in the cochlea. Hearing sensitivity for low frequency sounds related best to the condition of the hair cells in the apical region of the cochlea, while sensitivity for high frequency sound related best to the condition of the cells near the base of the cochlea. However, while a loss of 20 percent of the hair cells in the apical region of the cochlea resulted in no well-defined loss of hearing sensitivity, the loss of 10 to 20 percent of the cells in the basal region of the cochlea seemed to result in a hearing loss of up to 40 dB for high frequency sounds. This region also appears to be more susceptible to damage because resonances in the outer ear canal apparently amplify the intensity of sounds with frequencies near 4,000 Hz. These two factors are apparently responsible for the rather sharp drop in hearing sensitivity at 4,000 Hz frequently observed in people who have been exposed to noise. Noise-induced hearing loss is a function of three main factors: (1) overall noise level, (2) the frequency compositions of the noise, and (3) the total duration of exposure. Even moderate levels of industrial noise can therefore cause hearing loss if the individual is exposed to such noise eight hours a day for a period of many years.[5]

The relationship between industrial noise and hearing loss has been well established. For example in one study on 400 men and 90 women whose history of exposure to noise was known and who had worked for twelve years in an environment where the noise level was about 90 dB in each of the six octave frequency bands between 150 and 9,600 Hz [95 dB(A)], the measured hearing losses averaged 7 dB at 2,000 Hz, 27 dB at 3,000 Hz, and 40 dB at 4,000 Hz. Some of the men tested, even as young as thirty years of age, found difficulty in understanding speech after ten years' exposure to noise at this level.[6]

In 1967 the U.S. Public Health Service conducted a survey among operators of heavy earthmoving equipment (large dozers, scraper-loaders, compactors, etc.) on dam, canal, and roadbuilding projects. Noise from such equipment can be characterized as steady-state noise of a variable nature, since the intensity is not constant with time. Percentage time distributions of the observed A-scale sound level readings taken in the operator's compartment were made, and from these, equivalent continuous noise levels were calculated. These ranged from 92 to 117.5 dB(A) for the different pieces of equipment. In Figure 2-8, mean hearing levels of the workers in various age groups are compared with hearing levels of control groups of the same age and sex who have had no significant occupational noise exposure. The data clearly show that (1) In all age groups the equipment operators have significantly poorer hearing than the control groups who have had insignificant occupational noise exposure; and (2) Hearing loss increases with age for both groups, but the increase is much more marked in the case of the equipment operators.[7]

In the United States, responsibility for safety and health of employees is shared by the federal and state governments. Despite the fact that industrial noise has been a problem in certain industries for a great many years, only a few states in the United States have safety regulations which include noise exposure. Those that do, such as California, have generally chosen standards which are much too high. On May 20, 1969, the U.S. Department of Labor for the first time put into effect regulations for exposure of workers to industrial noise. Those regulations, known as the Walsh-Healy Health and Safety Regulations, applied only to those firms which have contracts with the federal government totalling $10,000 or more during any given year, and set 90 dB(A) as the maximum noise level to which workers may be exposed for an eight-hour day.

In 1970 Congress enacted the Occupational Safety and Health Act (Public Law 91-596) which requires the Secretary of Labor to establish and enforce

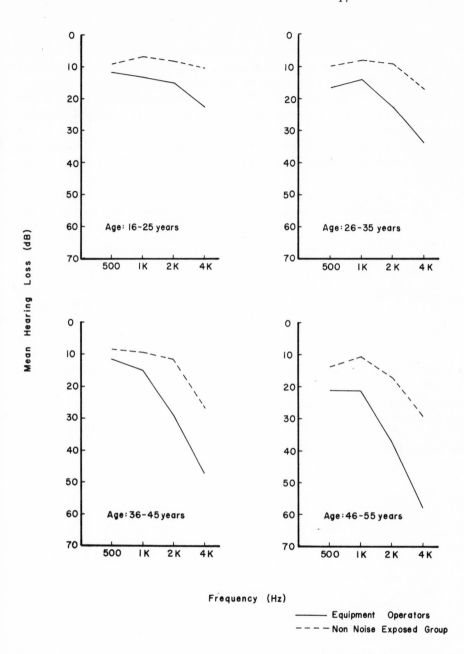

Figure 2-8. Comparison of Mean Hearing Levels of Heavy Equipment Operators with Control Groups with No Occupational Noise Exposure, by Age Group.[7]

mandatory safety and health standards applicable to employees of all businesses which affect interstate commerce. The Construction Safety Act (Public Law 91-54) requires the Secretary of Labor to prescribe safety and health standards for workers employed on a variety of federal and federally-assisted construction projects.[a] On May 29, 1971, the Secretary of Labor published in the *Federal Register* the noise exposure limitations he has promulgated under the new Occupational Safety and Health Act of 1970. These regulations, which are identical to the noise limitations prescribed under the Construction Safety Act and published in the *Federal Register* on April 17, 1971, are as follows:

Section 1910.95 Occupational Noise Exposure

(a) Protection against the effects of noise exposure shall be provided when the sound levels exceed those shown in Table G-16 when measured on the A scale of a standard sound level meter at slow response. (Note: this section also provides that noise levels may be determined by octave band analysis and converted to the equivalent A-weighted sound levels).

(b) (1) When employees are subjected to sound levels exceeding those listed in Table G-16, feasible administrative or engineering controls shall be utilized. If such controls fail to reduce sound levels within the levels of Table G-16, personal protective equipment shall be provided and used to reduce sound levels within the levels of the table.
(2) If the variations in noise level involve maxima at intervals of 1 second or less, it is to be considered continuous.
(3) In all cases where the sound levels exceed the values shown herein, a continuing, effective hearing conservation program shall be administered.

Table G-16
Permissible Noise Exposures*

Duration per day (hours)	Sound Level dB(A) slow response
8	90
6	92
4	95
3	97
2	100
1½	102
1	105
½	110
¼ or less	115

*When the daily noise exposure is composed of two or more periods of noise exposure of different levels, their combined effect should be considered, rather than the individual effect of each. If the sum of the following fractions,

$$\frac{C_1}{T_1} + \frac{C_2}{T_2} + \ldots + \frac{C_n}{T_n}$$

exceeds unity, then the mixed exposure should be considered to exceed the limit value. C_n indicates the total time of exposure at a specified noise level, and T_n indicates the total time of exposure permitted at that level.

Exposure to impulsive or impact noise should not exceed 140 dB peak sound pressure level.

[a]For information on construction projects subject to these regulations, the interested reader should consult reference 8 at the end of this chapter.

Even though hearing losses have been shown to occur from exposure to 80 dB(A) over a period of many years, these new standards afford no more protection to the worker than the old Walsh-Healy regulations which they superseded. It is interesting to note that in January 1969, the outgoing Johnson Administration proposed noise standards which would have limited exposure to 85 dB(A) for an eight-hour work day. In March 1971, the late congressman William Ryan (D., N.Y.) and 35 other members of the House introduced legislation which would have required the Secretary of Labor to reduce each of the maximum permissible noise levels in Table G-16 by 10 dB(A). Under the terms of this bill, the maximum permissible noise level for an eight-hour exposure would have been 80 dB(A). Unfortunately, Ryan's bill was never enacted.

In Canada, responsibility for the safety and health of employees is divided between the federal and provincial governments. In general, activities which fall within federal jurisdiction are somewhat more restricted than in the United States. Broadly speaking, these activities and enterprises include interprovincial and international railways, highway transport, shipping and shipping services, canals, ferries, tunnels and bridges, pipelines, telephone, telegraph and cable systems. They also include radio and television broadcasting, air transport, banks, grain elevators, flour and feed mills, feed warehouses, grain seed cleaning plants, and certain Crown corporations. The balance of industries and businesses are under the jurisdiction of the provincial governments.

Although most of the provinces have a noise control requirement in their industrial safety regulations, they too have generally chosen standards which are too high.

Under Part IV of the Canada Labor Code, the Minister of Labor promulgated noise control regulations for industries subject to federal jurisdiction. These regulations were published as SOR/71-584 in the *Canada Gazette* on November 24, 1971. These regulations specify that sound levels be determined using the slow meter response on a sound level meter equipped with an A-weighting network or determined by an octave band analysis and converted to the equivalent A-weighted sound levels.

Section 3 of these regulations provides:

3. (1) Subject to subsections (2) and (3), no employer shall permit any of his employees to work at a site where the sound level is 90 dB(A) or more.
   (2) Where it is not reasonably practicable for an employer to comply with subsection (1), that employer may permit any employee to work at a site where he is exposed each day to
      (a) a sound level set out in Column I of the Schedule for a number of hours not exceeding the number set out in Column II of the Schedule opposite that sound level; or
      (b) a number of different sound levels, set out in Column I of the Schedule, if the sum of the quotients resulting from the division of
         (i) the number of hours of exposure to each sound level, by
         (ii) the maximum number of hours of exposure per work day set

out in Column II of the Schedule opposite each such sound level does not exceed one.

Schedule
Maximum permitted noise exposure at a work site

Column I Sound level in dB(A)	Column II Maximum number of hours of exposure per work day
90 or more but less than 92	8
92 or more but less than 95	6
95 or more but less than 97	4
97 or more but less than 100	3
100 or more but less than 102	2
102 or more but less than 105	1½
105 or more but less than 107	1
107 or more but less than 110	¾
110 or more but less than 112	½
112 or more but less than 115	¼
115 or more	0

Section 3. (3) permits an employer to allow employees to work at a site where the sound level is 90 dB(A) or more if it is not reasonably practicable for an employer to comply with subsections (1) or (2) above provided that the employee is provided with and wears a hearing protector that reduces the sound level reaching his ears to less than 90 dB(A).

Section 4 of the regulations even permits an employee to work without hearing protectors at a site where the noise level to which he is exposed is 90 to 95 dB(A) if

. . . a test of the hearing of that employee established that he can, without any impairment of hearing, work at that site; and the employee's hearing level is tested regularly at such intervals as may be required by the Division Chief.

These regulations are clearly more lax than even the U.S. federal standards. Section 4 is particularly undesirable because, in the case of a single individual, it is not always possible to distinguish between occupationally-induced hearing loss and the hearing loss that accompanies aging. Consequently, there is a danger that occupationally-caused hearing loss will be dismissed as presbycusis—the hearing loss that accompanies aging.

In February 1972 a bill was introduced into the Canadian House of Commons which would limit the noise level in establishments having contracts with the Government of Canada to 85 dB(A). Although the measure was not enacted during the fourth session of the twenty-eighth Parliament, the bill's author, Barry Mather (N.D.P.,B.C) has stated that he plans to reintroduce it in the next session.

In a 1965 report, the Committee on Hearing, Bioacoustics, and Biomechanics of the U.S. National Academy of Science and National Research Council (CHABA) developed sets of noise exposure levels for the different octave bands of noise for various exposure times during an eight-hour work day that would result in a specified risk of damage. The exposure levels which the CHABA group adopted were designed to protect 80 percent of the workers exposed for a period of ten years to the maximum levels from a hearing loss so severe as to impair the understanding of speech. Some of the noise exposure contours, converted into tabular form, are shown in Table 2-1. Note that these noise exposure criteria are not adequate to prevent hearing loss; they merely give a certain probability that the hearing loss will not be so severe as to significantly impair the understanding of speech. This criterion allows a maximum hearing loss of about 10 dB at frequencies of 1,000 Hz or lower, 15 dB at 2,000 Hz, and 20 dB at 3,000 Hz and above. Furthermore, note that only about 80 percent of the population exposed to the allowable levels are assured of even this protection.

In Figure 2-8 we saw that even people who presumably had no significant occupational noise exposure suffered a loss of hearing with age. This phenomenon is called presbycusis and has been attributed to the effects of aging. The results of a study made on 2,518 professional men who had no occupational noise hazard exposure are shown in Figure 2-9. Clearly there was a progressive hearing loss with age and, furthermore, the hearing loss was greatest in the higher frequency ranges. This is precisely the type of loss observed in people who have suffered a hearing loss as a result of exposure to moderate or severe industrial noise. Recently, Dr. Samuel Rosen has found that Mabaan tribesmen, who live in a primitive society in the Sudan free of the noise characteristic of industrialized nations, retain remarkably good hearing at seventy to eighty years of age.[10] Thus, while loss of hearing with age was formerly thought to be merely a part of

Table 2-1
Damage Risk Criteria Developed by CHABA Expressed as Octave Band Sound Pressure Levels (in dB) as a Function of Exposure Time Per Day

Exposure Time per Day	Octave Band Center Frequency (Hz)						
	125	250	500	1000	2000	4000	8000
8 hrs.	96	92	88	86	85	85	86
4 hrs.	103	96	91	88	86	85	87
2 hrs.	110	101	94	91	88	87	90
1 hr.	118	107	99	95	91	90	95
30 min.	126	114	105	100	95	93	99
3 min.	135	135	134	124	113	111	120

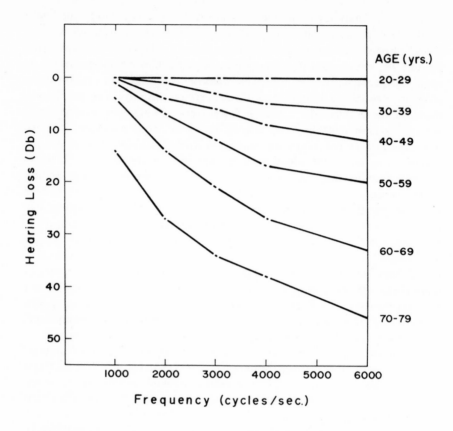

Figure 2-9. Average Hearing Loss, Shown as a Function of Frequency, in Different Age Groups Among 2,518 Professional Men Who Had No Occupational Noise Exposure.[6],[9]

the aging process, some evidence now suggests that environmental noise may be responsible for at least a portion of the hearing loss found in the U.S. population.

In addition to its potentially damaging effects on hearing and the sensory cells of the ear, noise can produce other physiological effects, the most important of which is probably its effect on sleep. Dr. Jerome Lukas of the Stanford Research Institute, Menlo Park, California, reported the results of some preliminary studies of the effects of aircraft noise and sonic booms on sleep at the American Medical Association's Sixth Congress on Environmental Health in Chicago, April 28-29, 1969. By making electroencephalogram recordings (EEG) of the brain wave activity and monitoring the rapid eye movements characteristic of light, dreamful sleep through electronystagmography (ENG), Dr. Lukas was able to observe the physiological effects of aircraft noise and sonic booms on the subjects. The subjects were exposed to simulated sonic booms and recorded flyover noise from subsonic fanjet aircraft of different intensities while in various stages of sleep. Significantly, many of the subjects, particularly those of middle age, began complaining of excessive fatigue in the mornings even though they had not been fully awakened more than twice during the night by the noise stimuli. The EEG and ENG data showed, however, that the noise stimuli often roused them from a deep dreamless sleep to a lighter, but still sub-arousal stage. The data indicate, therefore, that complete arousal is by no means necessary to produce feelings of fatigue.[11]

Other extra-auditory physiological effects have been found by a number of European investigators. Dr. Gerd Jansen of the Ruhr University, Essen, West Germany, reported at a conference sponsored by the American Speech and Hearing Association and the U.S. Public Health Service in Washington, D.C., February, 1969, that broadband noise with an overall intensity level as low as 70 dB produced pupil dilation and vasoconstriction. These effects increased with the intensity level of the noise and seemed to be independent of annoyance or other emotional reactions. Whether high noise levels over a long period of time can cause permanent effects of this nature is not yet clear. But as Dr. Jansen pointed out, "If there is an additional psychic or somatic stress, human health might be endangered even by lower intensities and shorter exposure time."[12]

In addition to the physiological effects we have discussed, there are a myriad of psychological effects which have never been adequately documented much less quantified. We have all felt annoyance, irritation, and frustration at the intrusion of unwanted sounds into our lives and the privacy of our homes, but how does one measure such effects?

From studies conducted thus far, some broad generalizations can be made. Intensity level is a factor, although not necessarily the most important one, in the degree of annoyance caused by a particular noise. A high frequency noise is generally more annoying than one of low frequency, and a noise in which an appreciable fraction of the sound energy is contained in pure tone or narrow band components is more annoying than broad band noise. However, the degree of annoyance caused by a noise depends greatly on what we are trying to do at the moment, and individuals differ in their tolerance of noise. From studies that have been made on work output, quality rather than quantity appears to be affected most by noise. Although noise may not significantly reduce total work output, it results in more errors. Noise also results in marked fluctuations in performance. Thus, performance on tasks requiring careful and continuous vigilance is most susceptible to impairment. For these reasons, attempts to devise rating scales for annoyance have not met with much success. Even if a scale for annoyance could somehow be devised, how does one rate the effect of such annoyance on the decisions of the corporate executive or the productivity of the trained scientific mind?

Finally, a subject of some concern in the area of psychological effects is dream deprivation. In the previously discussed work of Dr. Jerome Lukas, noise sometimes resulted in dream termination without the subject necessarily being awakened. Other studies have also demonstrated that dreaming is necessary for mental health. Consequently, dream deprivation caused by noise could have significant long-term effects on the mental health of large populations.

While direct causal relations between noise and psychosocial problems are difficult to prove because of confounding and frequently unknown factors in the populations under study, we can conclude with reasonable certainty that limits for environmental noise sources cannot be set by adhering only to physiologically safe levels because such levels would frequently result in great mental distress.

In 1958, Leroy Burney, then U.S. Surgeon General, called the First National Conference on Air Pollution in Washington, D.C., and in his opening remarks he made this observation:

Referring to the circumstantial evidence relating cancer to atmospheric pollution, I remarked that the case has not yet been proved. This legal metaphor is frequently used. I submit to you that it is misleading. In law, the suspect is innocent until his guilt has been proved beyond reasonable doubt. In the protection of human health, such absolute proof often comes late. To wait for it is to invite disaster, or at least to suffer unnecessarily through long periods of time.[13]

In its noteworthy report, *Toward a Quieter City*, the Mayor's Task Force on Noise Control of New York City stated,

The evidence is indeed overwhelming that to label unwelcome noise, a benign nuisance is a disservice to the rights of the individual. Anxiety, constrained and explosive rage, disturbed sleep, irritability, and concentration and energy draining tensions, are direct and preventable results of noise in our community. They are clinically, if not statistically, demonstrable and, in terms of the mental health of our community, should be attacked through legislative and educative measures.[14]

Sources of Noise and Their Control

In our technological age the sources of noise seem almost infinite. From the kitchen in the modern dwelling comes a cacophony that, were the exposure for an eight-hour working day, would be sufficient to cause hearing impairment. Radios, TVs, vacuum cleaners, power lawn mowers, and outside air conditioners add to the din in the home.

Because of the paper-thin walls in most new apartment buildings, today's apartment dweller is frequently assaulted by the noise from his neighbor's appliances as well as his own. In some communities, intrusion of noise from nearby industrial areas is a serious problem. But in most of the world's major metropolitan areas construction and transportation sources, particularly trucks, motorcycles, sports cars, and aircraft (both civil and military) are the most serious offenders.

In matters related to noise pollution, as in air and water pollution problems, economic considerations have generally taken precedence over environmental considerations. Furthermore, the machines that make noise frequently benefit certain groups of people while imposing the noise nuisance on another group that does not share in the benefits. As we shall see, an outstanding example of this situation is found in the problem of aircraft noise. Unfortunately, the technical aspects of noise have been understood and utilized much more effectively by industry than by the public. Indeed, for much of the noise legislation now on the books in the United States and Canada the criteria and measurements have been provided by the industries to be regulated with some assistance from certain technical societies. Consequently, the criteria or standards specified in such legislation have rarely been adequate to provide any significant measure of protection to the public.

The Noise Control Act of 1972 (Public Law 92-574), for the first time, requires the administrator of the U.S. Environmental Protection Agency (EPA) to publish a report identifying the products (or classes of products) which constitute major noise sources and to set noise emission standards for such products. Noise emission regulations may also be established for other products for which the EPA administrator deems noise emission standards to be feasible and which fall into one of the following categories: (1) construction equipment; (2) transportational equipment (including recreational vehicles); (3) any motor or engine (including any equipment of which an engine is an integral part); and (4) electrical or electronic equipment. The term "product" specifically excludes aircraft and related components which are treated separately under the Act (see Chapter 6).[15,16,17]

The major regulatory thrust of this legislation is a requirement for the administrator of EPA to establish noise emission standards for newly manufactured products that are deemed to be major sources of noise on the theory that federal regulation is needed to effectively control noise from motor vehicles, construction equipment, and other machinery which move freely in interstate commerce. Noise emission standards established by EPA would apply only to new products manufactured after the effective date of the standards. Since this new law also requires the EPA administrator to allow interested persons to participate in establishment of any regulatory standards, public participation in the rule-making process will be essential if the standards are not to reflect the interests of the affected industries.

The Noise Control Act also contains a federal preemption clause which, in the case of products for which a noise emission standard has been set by EPA, prohibits a state or local government from establishing or enforcing a standard different from the federal one. State and local governments do, however, retain authority to establish and enforce limits on environmental noise through licensing, regulation, or restriction of the use or operation of vehicles, equipment, or other products. Other aspects of this new legislation will be discussed in subsequent chapters.

3 Noise in Dwellings

At some time we have all experienced difficulty in understanding conversation because of high noise levels. Speech sounds that lie between 200 and 6,000 Hz contain nearly all the information necessary for the understanding of spoken English, and about one-half of the information lies on either side of 1,650 Hz. Noise of sufficient intensity to effectively mask part of the sounds within this frequency range interferes with the intelligibility of speech.

Some noises, such as those of motor vehicular traffic, turbojet aircraft, escaping air, and many household appliances are known as continuous spectrum noises because the sound energy is distributed over a broad range of frequencies. Dr. Leo Beranek has developed an approximate measure of the masking effect of such continuous spectrum noises on speech. The masking effect of the intruding noise is designated as the Speech Interference Level (SIL) defined as the simple arithmetic average of the sound pressure levels in the three octave bands centered on 500, 1,000, and 2,000 Hz. One can use the SIL to ascertain the conditions under which speech communication is relatively easy, difficult, or impossible. For example, we see from Table 3-1 that if the SIL is 74 dB, the speaker has to shout to make himself understood at a distance of 4 feet.

From these Speech Interference Levels, criteria have been established for background noise levels in homes, offices, schools, indeed all types of structures in which speech communication is essential. Criteria developed by Beranek for a few structures are shown in Table 3-2. The utility of these criteria can be

Table 3-1
Speech Interference Levels of Intruding Noise[1]

Distance Between Speaker and Listener in Feet	Speech Interference Level (Arithmetic Average of the Sound Pressure Levels in 3 Octave Bands Centered on 500, 1,000, and 2,000 Hz).			
	Voice Levels			
	Normal	Raised	Very Loud	Shouting
1	68	74	80	86
2	62	68	74	80
4	56	62	68	74
6	52	58	64	70
12	46	52	58	64

27

Table 3-2
Recommended Limits for Noise in Rooms

Type of Space	Recommended Maximum SIL
Small private office	30-40
Small conference room (20 people)	30-40
Large conference room (50 people)	25-35
Clerical offices, drafting rooms	40-55
School rooms	30
Homes	30-40

realized if we suppose that one wishes to locate a small conference room in an industrial plant. If the noise level in the three octave bands centered on 500, 1,000, and 2,000 Hz is measured in the plant at the location of the proposed conference room and the average is found to be 70 dB, the conference room must be constructed in such a manner that an attenuation of about 35 dB is provided in order to have a room with a satisfactory background noise level.

Direct translation of Speech Interference Levels into easily measured dB(A) values cannot be made unless the noise spectrum is known. However, as a general precaution against spectral peaking in the SIL bands, one should not allow the measured dB(A) levels to exceed the SIL criteria by more than 5 dB. Thus, if one wants to hold the SIL to a maximum of 35 dB, the A-weighted sound level should not be permitted to exceed 40 dB(A).

In the home, if normal conversation, or the radio or TV, operating at moderate levels, is to be comfortably understood, the background noise should not exceed an SIL of 30 to 40 dB. From the above guidelines, we see that these criteria mean the A-weighted sound levels should not exceed 35 to 45 dB(A). Note, however, that these are maximum noise levels for the clear intelligibility of speech. In fact, the background noise level at night in a quiet home in a suburban residential area well removed from arterial or freeway traffic is often only 20-25 dB(A). Unfortunately, few modern dwellings are as quiet. Some architectural designs combined with cheap construction turn many modern dwellings into acoustic disasters. We have already seen that some home appliances are extremely noisy devices. The unsatisfactory design, inferior materials, and poor construction of many homes makes escape from the noise impossible.

The problem is especially acute in most modern apartments where, because of the single walls and single-layer floors between units, the occupant is assaulted by the noise from adjacent units as well as from exterior sources. Surveys have shown that the most prevalent noise complaints among apartment dwellers involve the transmission of noise from one apartment to another within the building. The most frequently cited noise sources are television, radio or stereo sets, occupant activity, plumbing systems, household appliances, and electro-mechanical equipment such as pumps, ventilating fans, heating or air condition-ing systems, and elevators.

Major property management firms report that noise transmission is one of the most serious problems facing apartment building managers. Both managers and owners of apartment buildings admit that lack of both acoustical privacy and noise control is one of the greatest detractions to apartment living and that as a result of noise transmission, market resistance is increasing. Because of the very poor sound insulation, many of the new high-rise apartment buildings in New York have occupancy factors below the profit margin for the owner. The problem is aggravated during the summer months because of the noise from window air conditioners.

Most noise transmission problems in both single family and multifamily dwellings can be attributed to the following factors:

1. Lightweight building structures. Chiefly because of their lower cost, the partition walls and the floor-ceiling assemblies used in both home and apartment construction today are lighter weight and hence less effective sound insulators than those employed in the past.
2. Poor acoustical design. Many noise problems arise as a result of poor choice of building location or orientation, use of large-area windows which front on major traffic arteries or other noisy areas, design and layout of interior rooms without proper regard for noise sources within the building, and poor acoustical design in plumbing, heating, and air conditioning systems.
3. Poor workmanship. Unfortunately, the use of materials with good acoustical performance is too often negated by poor workmanship on the part of the building contractor or craftsmen, particularly in the installation of equipment or appliances, pipes, ducts, electrical outlets, cabinets, and plumbing fixtures.
4. Household appliances. Labor-saving devices, particularly in the kitchen, continue to proliferate. Unfortunately, some of these devices, such as garbage disposals and food blenders, are extremely noisy, and as yet, little attention has been given to noise reduction in appliances.
5. Increasing density. Replacement of old, single-family residences with high density multiple dwellings in highly urbanized areas has led not only to a great increase in population density in such areas, but also to an enormous increase in motor vehicle traffic. As a consequence, not only are families living in closer physical proximity to each other, but both exterior and interior noise levels have increased substantially.
6. Perhaps the most fundamental problem is the inadequate level of financial support devoted to acoustical research and the lack of adequate acoustical training provided planners, transportation system designers, city adminis-trators, equipment and appliance manufacturers, and people associated with the building industry.

The technical knowledge and means for producing quiet housing exist. Their application has been impeded, however, by economic and political considerations. Quiet housing obviously costs more, though precisely how much more is somewhat uncertain, since there appears to be relatively little reliable information on which to base an estimate. With a basic design that takes into account ambient noise patterns, the cost of soundproofing for a single-family home compared to none at all is $500 to $1,000. Estimates for apartment buildings indicate that the actual cost differential between an apartment building with good acoustical design and soundproofing versus one with none might vary between 2 and 10 percent of the cost of the building depending on size, location, labor market, etc. To the prospective tenant, however, a new but cheaply built apartment does not appear greatly different from one in which higher quality materials and workmanship were used and which is soundproofed. Consequently, the owner of the cheaply constructed apartment is able to collect, for a short time at least, almost as much rent as is the owner of an adequately soundproofed building, despite the fact his investment is somewhat less. Not until the new tenant has signed a lease, perhaps, does he discover the inferior acoustical properties of the building.

Although proper acoustical design and sound insulation results in an added initial cost of the building, the additional expenses are often far less than those required to remedy serious acoustical problems in a completed building. In the latter case, major redesign and reconstruction of partition walls or floor-ceiling assemblies may be needed to solve the problem.

The obvious answer is the enactment of noise control requirements in building codes. Since each city in both the United States and Canada writes its own building code, there is a considerable lack of uniformity among building codes—a fact which builders and speculators use to their own advantage. Furthermore, few cities in either the United States or Canada have building codes which contain noise control requirements, although an increasing number of Canadian cities are adopting the 1970 National Building Code of Canada which does contain some sound insulation requirements.

Writing a well-conceived building code which specifies airborne sound and impact isolation is not an easy task. One might suppose that a building code which specified certain types of partition walls and floor-ceiling assemblies together with a catalogue of noise ratings for the various wall and floor constructions would suffice. Unfortunately, such is not the case. Transmission of sound from one room to an adjacent room separated by a partition wall may occur directly through the wall or by indirect paths. Noise transmission through indirect paths is frequently called "flanking transmission" and for airborne noise may occur through heating or air conditioning ducts, open ceiling plenums which span both rooms, or common corridors. Flanking transmission paths also occur as a result of back-to-back installation of cabinets and electrical outlets, failure to seal pipe and conduit penetrations through a partition wall, and poor seals between partition walls and floors or ceilings.

Flanking paths for structure-borne noise are numerous and often difficult to trace, but the primary flanking path is the skeletal structure of the building. Vibrational energy from fans, pumps, appliances, heating or air conditioning units, plumbing systems, and occupant activity is often transmitted to the building structure and then carried with little attenuation to walls and floors throughout the building, from which it is radiated as airborne sound. Obviously, use of high performance acoustical materials will not provide the desired sound insulation if they are "short circuited" by flanking transmission paths.

The effectiveness of airborne sound isolation is usually determined from noise measurements made in two adjacent rooms separated by a partition. Until fairly recently, such measurements were made in the six octave frequency bands, 125, 250, 500, 1,000, 2,000, and 4,000 Hz. Today, however, analyses in 16 frequencies at one-third octave intervals covering the frequency range 125 to 4,000 Hz are preferred and there is a trend toward standardization of the one-third octave band analysis.

Laboratory measurements of the sound insulation properties of a partition wall or floor-ceiling assembly for airborne sound are commonly conducted according to the procedure recommended in the American Society for Testing and Materials E90-66T (see references at end of chapter). Two reverberant rooms are separated by the partition under test. A diffuse noise field is set up in one room and measured in both rooms. From these measurements plus a measurement of the sound absorption in the second room, the sound transmission loss (STL) of the partition under test can be calculated from the relation

$$STL = L_1 - L_2 + 10 \log S/A$$

where L_1 and L_2 are the average sound pressure levels in each frequency band, in decibels, measured in the source and receiving rooms respectively, S is the total radiating surface area of the partition, and A is the total sound absorption in the receiving room (expressed in square feet or square meters).[2,3,4,5]

When the sound transmission loss determined for each frequency band (preferably in one-third octave bands) is plotted against the band center frequency, a curve, called the sound transmission loss curve, results, which discloses the acoustical performance of the partition at each frequency. In Figures 3-1 to 3-3, STL curves for four different partition wall constructions are shown. The higher the curve falls on the graph, the better is the acoustical performance of the construction.

Of the constructions shown in the figures, the partition consisting of gypsum board nailed to wooden studs, which is very widely used today in both single-family and multiple dwellings, has the most inferior acoustical properties. Because of the rigid ties between the stud framing and the wall surfaces, vibrational excitation is readily transmitted from one wall surface to the other. Consequently, use of sound absorbing blanket material in the voids between studs provides very little improvement. A wall constructed of gypsum board

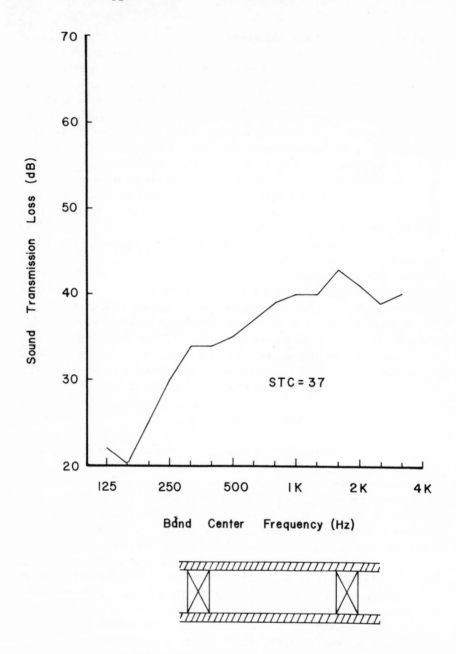

Figure 3-1. Sound Transmission Loss Curve for a Wall Consisting of ½-Inch Gypsum Wallboard. Note: The ½ inch gypsum wallboard is nailed to both sides of 2 x 4-inch wooden studs 16 inches on centers, with all joints taped and finished.[2]

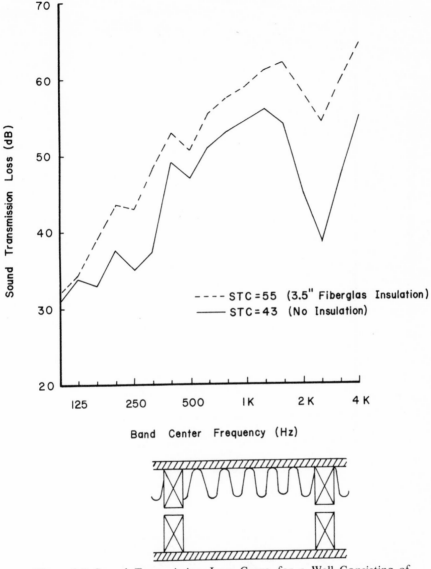

Figure 3-2. Sound Transmission Loss Curve for a Wall Consisting of 5/8-Inch Gypsum Board. Source: *Solutions to Noise Control Problems in Apartments, Motels and Hotels.* Reproduced with permission of Owens-Corning Fiberglas Corp. Note: The 5/8-inch gypsum board is on separate rows of 2 x 4-inch wooden studs, 16 inches on center, secured to separate 2 x 4-inch base plates. All joints taped and sealed and the joints along the floor and ceiling caulked. With no insulation, the STC is 43. If 3½ inches of Fiberglas building insulation is placed between studs, STC is raised to 55.

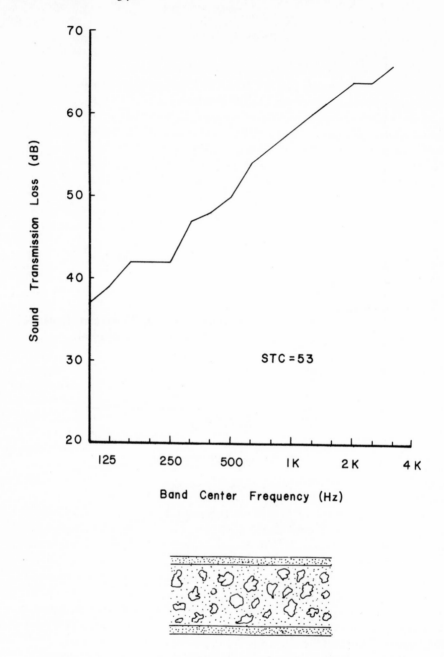

Figure 3-3. Sound Transmission Loss Curve for a 6-Inch Thick Concrete Wall Faced with a ½-Inch Thick Layer of Plaster on Both Sides.[2]

nailed to a double row of wooden studs gives much better acoustical performance, and if 3-1/2 inches of Fiberglas building insulation is installed vertically in
the stud space (see Figure 3-2) the acoustical performance is slightly superior to
that of a 7-inch thick solid concrete wall. Only by examining the STL curve can
one accurately assess the sound insulating value of a construction for a given
application. Nevertheless, single-figure ratings of airborne sound insulation have
gained considerable favor among architects, builders, and code writers because of
their simplicity. In recent years the most widely used single-figure rating system
has been the Sound Transmission Class (STC), which is based upon the test
procedure specified in ASTM E90-66T for laboratory measurement of sound
transmission loss. The STC of a partition is found by comparing the sound
transmission loss curve, determined from one-third octave band measurements
made over the frequency range 125-4,000 Hz, with a reference contour. The
reference contour is shifted vertically relative to the test curve to as high a
position as possible while still meeting the following two conditions:

1. The maximum deviation of the test curve below the reference contour may
   not exceed 8 dB at a single test frequency.
2. The sum of the deviations of the test curve below the reference contour at all
   sixteen test frequencies may not exceed 32 dB.

When the reference contour has been adjusted in this manner (in integral
decibels), the STC is read from the vertical scale on the graph and is numerically
equal to the STL value which corresponds to the intersection of the reference
contour and the 500 Hz line. The STC for the test curve shown in Figure 3-4 is
46. In this example, the placement of the reference contour is controlled by the
8 dB deviation at 2,500 Hz rather than by the second condition which limits the
sum of the deviations. In practice, positioning of the reference contour is usually
done with the aid of a transparent overlay. In Figures 3-1 to 3-3, the STC value
for each construction is also listed.

As an example of the use of such rating systems, let us consider the following
hypothetical situation. Suppose that two families occupy adjacent units, A and
B, in an apartment house located in a suburban residential area where the
exterior ambient nighttime noise level is 35-40 dB(A). Let us suppose that the
nighttime background noise level in the bedroom of Apartment A is represented
by curve (1) in Figure 3-5. This curve yields an A-weighted noise level of 31
dB(A). Let us also suppose that while the husband of Apartment A works a
normal 8 A.M. to 5 P.M. workday, both husband and wife of Apartment B work
the night shift and arrive home at about 1 A.M., whereupon they prepare a meal.
Let us further suppose that the bedroom of Apartment A is situated adjacent to
the kitchen of Apartment B. If the sleeping occupants of Apartment A are not
to be disturbed by the activity in the kitchen of Apartment B, then the partition
wall must be capable of reducing the transmitted noise to the level of the

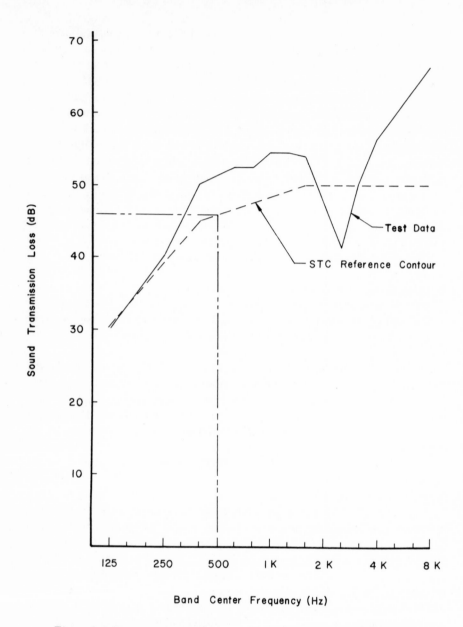

Figure 3-4. Determination of Sound Transmission Class (STC) by Comparison of the Sound Transmission Loss Curve, Determined from 1/3-Octave Band Measurements, with a Reference Contour. Source: *Solutions to Noise Control Problems in Apartments, Motels and Hotels*. Reproduced with permission of Owens-Corning Fiberglas Corp. Note: STC for the test data curve is 46.

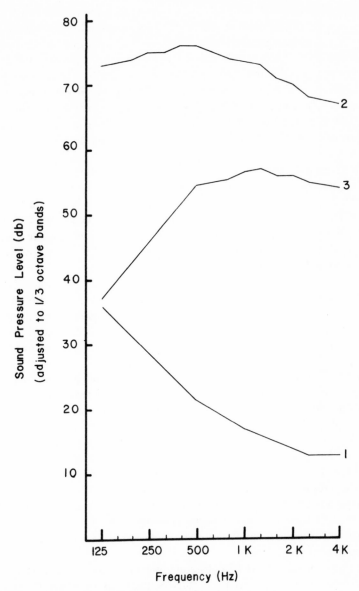

Frequency (Hz)

(3) Sound pressure level difference. (no. 2 minus no. 1)
(2) Assumed maximum noise level in kitchen.
(1) Interior night-time ambient noise level.

Figure 3-5. Example of a Determination of the Required Airborne Sound Insulating Properties of a Partition Wall Separating the Bedroom of One Apartment from the Kitchen of an Adjacent Unit.

background noise in the bedroom of Apartment A. If the transmitted noise level is less than the background, it will be effectively masked by the background and hence be inaudible. Suppose that the noise level produced in the kitchen of Apartment B is represented by curve (2) in Figure 3-5. Subtraction of curve (1) from curve (2) yields the sound pressure level differences [curve (3)] required for attenuation of the noise to the desired level. If one neglects the correction for sound absorption in the rooms, then curve (3) may be taken as an approximate sound transmission loss curve from which we can determine that the required partition must have an STC value of approximately 56 if it is to provide the necessary sound insulation.

The foregoing example also raises the question of using background noise to mask disturbing sounds. One might reason from this example that higher background noise levels in the bedroom would permit use of wall partitions with lower STC values. Up to the point at which the background noise itself becomes objectionable this may be true. However, use of background noise for masking is fraught with numerous difficulties. Background noise is nearly always broad-band noise and hence it will not effectively mask sounds which have appreciable pure-tone components. Furthermore, if the background noise itself is not to be disturbing, it should not only be broad-band noise, but should also be smooth, continuous, and essentially nondirectional. These requirements exclude noise from street traffic which, especially at night, is rarely continuous and often interrupted by trucks. Noise from furnace or air conditioner blowers is also excluded because these sources are cyclic in nature.

Use of background noise for masking purposes poses other difficulties. For example, exterior noise sources may result in higher interior background noise levels on one side of an apartment building than on the shielded side. If an acoustically inferior partition wall separates units on opposite sides of the building, occupants on the quiet side, deprived of the masking effect, would find the noise from the occupants in the adjacent unit quite annoying. Also, use of high background noise levels to compensate for acoustically inferior construction may result in people increasing the volume of their TV sets, thereby offsetting any beneficial masking effect. Introduction of masking noise may have some beneficial use in rendering noises of a temporary or intermittent nature less audible, but it is rarely an effective substitute for good acoustical insulation in new residential construction.

Measurement and control of structure-borne noise are more difficult than for airborne sound, in part because of the multitude of sources and transmission paths and also because no standardized test procedure has yet been devised. The International Organization for Standardization has developed a procedure, which is now used in some European countries, for the laboratory and field measurement of impact noise isolation of floor-ceiling structures. In this test procedure a so-called "standard tapping machine" is placed on the floor and the sound pressure levels generated in the room beneath the floor-ceiling structure are measured, usually in one-third octave band widths. A correction must also be applied for the total sound absorption in the receiving room. This so-called "standard tapping machine" consists of five hammers, spread about three inches apart and placed in a line, which fall to the floor in succession and create about 10 impacts per second. Each hammer weighs about 1.1 pounds and falls a distance of about 1.6 inches. Since the tapping machine does not simulate walking or any other recognizable occupant activity, there is presently some disagreement over the significance of the results obtained from such measurements. Nevertheless, this is the only reasonably well-standardized procedure for the measurement of impact noise isolation presently in use.

Because the frequency distribution of transmitted impact noise is an important consideration, impact noise isolation effectiveness of floor-ceiling structures should be determined on the basis of the entire impact sound pressure level curve. Because of their utility for providing general categories for different floor-ceiling structures and because of some interest on the part of code writers, single-figure rating systems have been devised for rating the impact noise insulation of structures. The older system is called the Impact Noise Rating (INR) and is based on the procedure given in ISO Recommendation R-140, *Field and Laboratory Measurements of Airborne and Impact Sound Transmission*. The sound pressure levels measured in one-third octave band widths in the room beneath the floor-ceiling structure on which the "standard tapping machine" is operating are adjusted to a reference room absorption of 10 m^2. The one-third octave band levels are then increased by 5 dB to represent the level that would result if full octave bands were used, and the resulting levels are then plotted against frequency at one-third octave intervals from 100 to 3,200 Hz. The INR is then determined by comparison of this curve with a reference contour (Figure 3-6). The reference contour is adjusted vertically with respect to the test curve to as low a position as possible such that the following two conditions are fulfilled:

1. The maximum deviation of the test curve above the reference contour may not exceed 8 dB at any single test frequency.
2. The sum of the deviations of the test curve above the reference contour at all sixteen test frequencies may not exceed 32 dB.[6]

When the reference contour has been thus adjusted with respect to the test curve, the INR value is determined by finding the octave band sound pressure level that corresponds to the intersection of the horizontal portion of the reference contour with the test curve and subtracting it from 66 dB. The U.S. Federal Housing Administration (FHA) has found that an INR of zero affords only marginally acceptable impact noise isolation. Positive values for the INR indicate better performance while negative values indicate poorer performance.

Some confusion has arisen over the fact that for airborne sound, high values

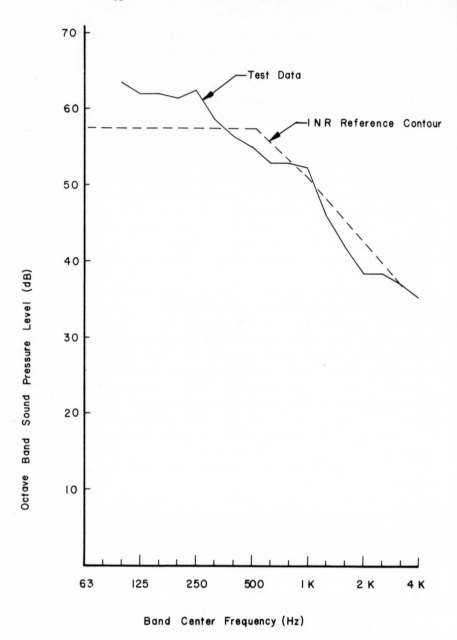

Figure 3-6. Determination of Impact Noise Rating (INR) by Comparison of Measured Sound Pressure Levels, Corrected to Full Octave Band Levels, with the INR Reference Contour. Source: *Solutions to Noise Control Problems in Apartments, Motels and Hotels.* Reproduced with permission of Owens-Corning Fiberglas Corp. Note: INR of the test data curve shown here is +9.

for sound transmission loss and hence also high STC values mean that a partition provides a high degree of sound attenuation, while high values for impact sound pressure levels, because the transmitted noise is measured directly in the room beneath the floor, mean poor impact insulation. To alleviate some of this confusion, the FHA has developed a new single-number rating system for impact noise isolation called Impact Insulation Class (IIC). The sound pressure level measurements, made at 16 frequencies between 100 and 3,200 Hz in one-third octave bands in the room beneath the floor-ceiling structure on which the "standard tapping machine" is operating are normalized to a reference room absorption of 10 m^2 and plotted against frequency. The resulting test curve is then compared to a reference contour by means of a transparent overlay, and the reference contour is positioned vertically relative to the test curve to as low a position as possible such that the following two conditions are fulfilled:

1. The maximum deviation of the test curve above the reference contour may not exceed 8 dB at any single frequency.
2. The sum of the deviations of the test curve above the reference contour at all sixteen frequencies may not exceed 32 dB.

A new vertical scale is drawn on the right-hand side of the graph (see Figure 3-7). Values on the new scale decrease with increasing one-third octave band sound pressure levels, and the two scales coincide only at 55 dB. To determine the IIC of the test structure one finds the value on the right-hand vertical scale that corresponds to the intersection of the reference contour and the 500 Hz line. Higher IIC values mean better acoustical performance, and in very general terms, equal numerical values for IIC and STC imply roughly equal insulating properties for impact noise and airborne sound.

The U.S. Federal Housing Administration has recommended airborne and impact sound insulation criteria for partitions separating dwelling units in multiple family dwellings, and these are set forth in the FHA's very comprehensive report, *A Guide to Airborne, Impact, and Structure Borne Noise Control in Multifamily Dwellings*. These criteria were developed for three different grades of housing which are distinguished from one another chiefly on the basis of the nighttime background noise levels.[2]

Grade I is applicable to suburban or quiet urban residential areas where the exterior nighttime noise levels are 35-40 dB(A). These criteria are also applicable to dwelling units above the eighth floor in high-rise buildings and to the better grade or "luxury" class apartments.

Grade II covers the largest group of apartments since it is applicable to suburban and urban residential areas which have average nighttime exterior noise levels of 40-45 dB(A).

Grade III criteria provide only minimal acoustical privacy and should be considered only for certain noisy locations where the exterior nighttime noise level is 55 dB(A) or higher.

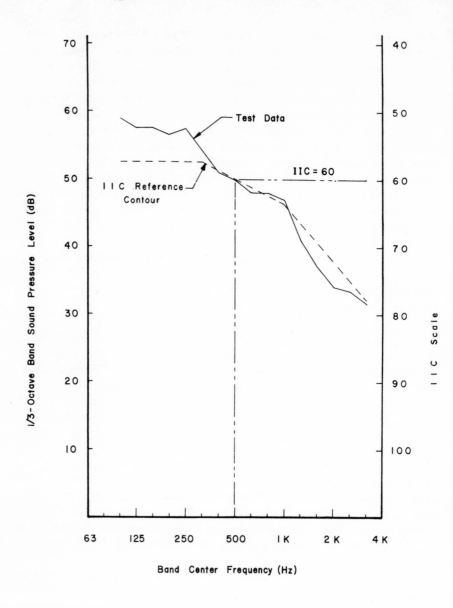

Figure 3-7. Determination of Impact Insulation Class (IIC) by Comparison of Measured Sound Pressure Levels with the IIC Reference Contour. Source: *Solutions to Noise Control Problems in Apartments, Motels and Hotels.* Reproduced with permission of Owens-Corning Fiberglas Corp.

The fundamental criteria for airborne and impact sound insulation of wall and floor-ceiling assemblies which *separate dwelling units of equivalent function* are given in Table 3-3. Tables 3-4 and 3-5 show the recommended STC and IIC values for partitions separating different functional spaces within a building. Of particular importance is the fact that these criteria are based upon STC and IIC ratings derived from laboratory measurements rather than field tests.

Unfortunately the criteria set forth above are merely recommendations, not requirements. While the United States does not have a national building code, the FHA has adopted construction standards with which builders are supposed to comply in order to qualify for FHA insured mortgages. For multiple-family dwellings, these standards are set forth in the FHA's *Minimum Property Standards for Multifamily Housing.* These minimum property standards contain no requirements for impact noise isolation. The requirements for airborne noise insulation between dwelling units are given in Table 3-6. We can readily see that these requirements for apartments in areas of low background noise are *less restrictive* than even the minimal Grade III criteria set forth in Table 3-4. Furthermore, even these so-called requirements are not necessarily mandatory, for the FHA report states,

It is not possible for one set of standards to encompass all conditions for all cost levels, in all geographic areas. For this reason these Minimum Property Standards are to be used as guides to aid the judgment of insuring office personnel in evaluating the quality of design and construction of the property which is to serve as security for an insured mortgage.

The application of sound transmission limitations to partitions, to floor and ceiling construction, and to suppression and isolation of mechanical noises and vibrations are mandatory. However, discretionary authority is given to FHA field officers to adapt the requirements herein to specific situations.[7]

In order to qualify for FHA insured mortgages, new single-family residences and duplexes are supposed to meet the construction standards set forth in the FHA's *Minimum Property Standards for One and Two Living Units.* Unfortunately, these minimum property standards contain no requirements for sound control in either construction or site planning. In fact, only one short paragraph is devoted to the whole subject of site planning. The only reference made to

Table 3-3
Fundamental Criteria for Airborne and Impact Sound Insulation of Partitions Separating Dwelling Units of Equivalent Function[2]

	Grade I	Grade II	Grade III
Wall Partitions	STC ⩾ 55	STC ⩾ 52	STC ⩾ 48
Floor-Ceiling Assemblies	STC ⩾ 55	STC ⩾ 52	STC ⩾ 48
	IIC ⩾ 55	IIC ⩾ 52	IIC ⩾ 48

Table 3-4

Criteria for Airborne Sound Insulation of Wall Partitions Separating Dwelling Units[2]

| Partition Separates | | | STC | |
Apt. A	Apt. B	Grade I	Grade II	Grade III
Bedroom	from Bedroom	55	52	48
Living room	from Bedroom[1,2]	57	54	50
Kitchen[3]	from Bedroom[1,2]	58	55	52
Bathroom	from Bedroom[1,2]	59	56	52
Corridor	from Bedroom[2,4]	55	52	48
Living room	from Living room	55	52	48
Kitchen[3]	from Living room[1,2]	55	52	48
Bathroom	from Living room[1]	57	54	50
Corridor	from Living room[2,4,5]	55	52	48
Kitchen	from Kitchen[6]	52	50	46
Bathroom	from Kitchen[1]	55	52	48
Corridor	from Kitchen[2,4,5]	55	52	48
Bathroom	from Bathroom	52	50	46
Corridor	from Bathroom[2,4]	50	48	46

[1]The most desirable plan would have the dwelling unit partition separating spaces with equivalent functions, e.g., living room opposite living room, etc.; however, when this arrangement is not feasible, the partition must have greater sound insulating properties.

[2]Whenever a partition wall might serve to separate several functional spaces, the highest criterion must prevail.

[3]Or dining, or family, or recreation room.

[4]It is assumed here that there is no entrance door leading from corridor to living unit.

[5]A common approach to corridor partition construction correctly assumes the entrance door as the acoustically weakest link and then incorrectly assumes that the basic partition wall need be no better acoustically than the door. However, the basic partition wall may separate the corridor from sensitive living areas such as the bedroom and bathroom without entrance doors, and must therefore have adequate insulating properties to assure acoustical privacy in these areas. In areas where entrance doors are used, the integrity of the corridor-living unit partition must be maintained by utilizing solid-core entrance doors with proper gasketing. The most desirable arrangement has the entrance door leading from the corridor to a partially enclosed vestibule or foyer in the living unit.

[6]Double-wall construction is recommended to provide, in addition to airborne sound insulation, isolation from impact noises generated by the placement of articles on pantry shelves and the slamming of cabinet doors. Party walls which utilize resilient spring elements to achieve good sound insulation may be used, providing wall cabinets are not mounted on them. It is not practical to use such walls for mounting of wall cabinets because the sound insulating performance of the walls can be easily short-circuited, unless specialized vibration isolation techniques are used.

noise isolation concerns the control of noise transmission from summer air conditioning equipment, and there is no firm requirement for that, only a guideline.[8]

Table 3-5

Criteria for Airborne and Impact Sound Insulation of Floor-Ceiling Assemblies Separating Dwelling Units[2]

Partition Separates		Grade I		Grade II		Grade III	
Apt. A	Apt B.	STC	IIC	STC	IIC	STC	IIC
Bedroom	above Bedroom	55	55	52	52	48	48
Living room	above Bedroom[1,2]	57	60	54	57	50	53
Kitchen[3]	above Bedroom[1,2]	58	65	55	62	52	58
Family room	above Bedroom[1,2]	60	65	56	62	52	58
Corridor	above Bedroom[1,2]	55	65	52	62	48	58
Bedroom	above Living room[4]	57	55	54	52	50	48
Living room	above Living room	55	55	52	52	48	48
Kitchen	above Living room[1,2]	55	60	52	57	48	53
Family room	above Living room[1,2]	58	62	54	60	52	56
Corridor	above Living room[1,2]	55	60	52	57	48	53
Bedroom	above Kitchen[1,4]	58	52	55	50	52	46
Living room	above Kitchen[1,4]	55	55	52	52	48	48
Kitchen	above Kitchen	52	55	50	52	46	48
Bathroom	above Kitchen[1,2]	55	55	52	52	48	48
Family room	above Kitchen[1,2]	55	60	52	58	48	54
Corridor	above Kitchen[1,2]	50	55	48	52	46	48
Bedroom	above Family room[1,4]	60	50	56	48	52	46
Living room	above Family room[1,4]	58	52	54	50	52	48
Kitchen	above Family room[1,4]	55	55	52	52	48	50
Bathroom	above Bathroom	52	52	50	50	48	48
Corridor	above Corridor	50	50	48	48	46	46

[1]The most desirable plan would have the floor-ceiling assembly separating spaces with equivalent functions, e.g., living room above living room, etc.; however, when this arrangement is not feasible the assembly must have greater acoustical insulating properties.
[2]This arrangement requires greater impact sound insulation than the converse, where a sensitive area is above a less sensitive area.
[3]Or dining, or family, or recreation room.
[4]This arrangement requires equivalent airborne sound insulation and perhaps less impact sound insulation than the converse.

The Noise Control Act of 1972 (Public Law 92-574) may eventually lead to the establishment of some meaningful noise isolation requirements by the FHA. This new legislation directs all federal agencies to carry out the programs within their control in such a manner as "to promote an environment for all Americans

Table 3-6

Requirements for Airborne Noise Insulation Between Dwelling Units Specified in FHA Minimum Property Standards for Multifamily Housing[7]

	STC			
	Low Background Noise Location		High Background Noise Location[1]	
Partition Separates	Bedroom Adjacent to Partition	Other Rooms Adjacent to Partition	Bedroom Adjacent to Partition	Other Rooms Adjacent to Partition
Living unit from living unit	50	45	45	40
Living unit from corridor[2]	45	40	40	40
Living unit from public space[3]	50	50	45	45
Living unit from service areas[4]	55	55	50	50

[1]For buildings with all-year air conditioning and for dwelling units located above the eighth floor in high-rise buildings, the columns for low background noise should be used.

[2]If corridor floors are not carpeted, these values should be increased by 5 dB.

[3]Public spaces include lobbies, storage rooms, stairways, laundries.

[4]Service areas include boiler rooms, mechanical equipment rooms, garages, elevator shafts, etc.

free from noise that jeopardizes their health or welfare." It further requires each federal agency to consult with the administrator of the Environmental Protection Agency (EPA) in prescribing standards or regulations respecting noise.[9]

In 1969, New York City adopted a new building code which contains noise control requirements for apartment buildings. Section C 26-1208.2 of the building code, entitled Acoustical Isolation of Dwelling Units, specifies the following requirements for airborne noise insulation:

1. Walls, partitions, and floor-ceiling constructions separating dwelling units from each other or from public halls, corridors, or stairs shall have a minimum sound transmission class (STC) rating of 45 for airborne noise. This requirement shall not apply to dwelling unit entrance doors. However, such doors shall fit closely and not be undercut. For permits issued after January 1, 1972, the STC required shall be 50 for airborne noise and dwelling unit entrance doors shall at that time have a minimum STC of 35.

This section also contains the following requirement for structure-borne noise insulation: "Floor-ceiling constructions separating dwelling units from each other or from public halls or corridors shall have a minimum impact noise rating (INR) of 0."

The code provides a catalogue of wall and floor ceiling assemblies with STC and INR ratings which may be used to determine conformance with the above section. However, the code also provides that in the event conditions indicate an installed construction does not satisfy the noise control requirements, field measurements must be taken to determine conformance. Field measurements may not fail to meet the STC or INR requirements by more than 2 points.

The code also sets maximum permissible sound power levels for mechanical equipment located both inside and outside the building (i.e., in yards, court-yards, or on roofs) and specifies that wall and floor-ceiling partitions separating boiler rooms from dwelling units must have a minimum STC rating of 50.

While adoption of this code represents a significant first step for New York, when the requirements set forth in the code are compared with the criteria presented earlier the inadequacies in the New York code become all too apparent. Furthermore, the provisions of the code do not apply to single or double-occupancy dwellings or to commercial structures of any type. Neither does the code contain any provisions for protection against exterior noises other than those generated by equipment associated with the building. The New York Mayor's Task Force believed such protection to be unfeasible, principally because insulation against such noise is negated when the windows are kept open. Instead, the Task Force recommended that the city develop a noise rating system for both old and new apartments. Field measurements would be made by city-approved laboratories, and apartment building owners would be responsible for obtaining noise rating certificates which prospective tenants could request.[10]

A number of Canadian cities are adopting the 1970 National Building Code of Canada, which contains noise control requirements, as their local Building Bylaw. This code, which was prepared by the National Research Council of Canada, is written in a manner suitable for adoption by local municipalities. Its provisions are also applicable to housing projects sponsored by the Central Mortgage and Housing Corporation.[11]

Section 3.3.4.7 of this code provides for sound control in buildings used for residential occupancy:

3.3.4.7 Walls and floors separating dwelling units shall be designed and con-structed to restrict sound transmission in conformance with Part 9 of this By-law.

The specific sound control requirements are given in Section 9.11:

9.11.1.1 Sound transmission class ratings for construction shall be determined in accordance with ASTM E-90-66T, "Laboratory Measurement of Airborne Sound Transmission Loss of Building Partitions."

9.11.2.1 Construction shall provide a sound transmission class rating of not less than 45 between dwelling units in the same building and between a dwelling unit and any space common to two or more dwelling units.

9.11.2.2 Every service room or space such as storage room, laundry, workshop or building maintenance room or garage serving more than one dwelling unit, shall be separated from the dwelling units by a construction providing a sound transmission class rating of not less than 45.

Included in the code is a list of wall and floor-ceiling assemblies which are deemed to satisfy the requirements of this code. In many respects this code is inferior to even the New York City Building Code, for it contains no requirements on impact noise insulation, and there are no provisions for field tests to determine conformance of completed construction with the airborne sound insulation requirements of Sections 9.11.2.1 and 9.11.2.2.

Good acoustical performance of a partition assembly in a laboratory test is no guarantee whatever that the completed construction, in which a nominally identical partition is used, will provide the desired sound isolation. Sound transmission losses for airborne sound are often 8 to 10 dB less in field determinations than those obtained from laboratory measurements on nominally identical partition assemblies.

A number of factors may be responsible for the discrepancies often found between laboratory and field measurements. Among these are:

1. Variable room size, sound diffusion, and sound absorption in rooms in completed construction.
2. Variable or high background noise levels which interfere with the measurements.
3. Modification of test procedures necessitated by the field installation.
4. Flanking paths for sound transmission.

All of the above factors tend to reduce the reproducibility of field measurements and increase the discrepancies between laboratory and field measurements. The most serious of these is the flanking transmission paths. The laboratory measurement differs fundamentally from the field installation in that in the latter case the partition under test is an integral part of the building structure. Hence flanking transmission paths for structure-borne noise exist through its structural ties to the rest of the building. In addition, flanking transmission paths for airborne noise frequently exist in the form of ducts, poorly sealed penetrations for pipes and electrical conduit, poorly placed electrical outlets, unsealed cracks along the joints between wall partitions and floor or ceiling structures, and unsealed entrance doors. In high-rise buildings, separations between wall partitions and floor or ceiling structures sometimes occur because of differential settlement of the foundation, differential thermal expansion of support columns, or movement caused by wind. Use of properly designed control joints which contain resilient gasket material can minimize this difficulty.

For these reasons, sound transmission loss values obtained from field

installations are sometimes substantially lower than those obtained from laboratory measurements on a nominally identical partition, where a carefully
constructed test specimen is sealed in a special opening between two massive,
reverberant rooms, usually constructed of concrete. Good agreement between
laboratory and field tests can be achieved, however, provided that the field
installation is done under carefully supervised workmanship and that the test
conditions conform as closely as possible to those recommended in ASTM
E90-66T. Under such conditions, agreement between field and laboratory
measurements of sound transmission loss values of 1 to 3 dB can be achieved and
agreement between the STC values will be 1 to 2 points.

A standardized test procedure for measurement of impact noise has not yet
been adopted. Furthermore, there is a fundamental difference between laboratory and field measurements of impact noise isolation. In laboratory measurements the test panel is structurally isolated from the walls of the receiving room
so that only noise transmitted through the test panel is measured. However,
when a floor-ceiling partition is installed in a building, it becomes an integral
part of the building structure and thus transmits impact noise to the walls of the
room below. Consequently, a floor-ceiling partition will usually show poorer
impact noise insulation under field conditions than in the laboratory. Only if the
floor-ceiling assembly is vibrationally decoupled from the rest of the building
can comparable values be expected. Although vibrational isolation is difficult to
achieve, the means for doing so are available. In one such construction a floated
floor (vibrationally decoupled from the side walls with resilient gasket material)
is placed on a structural support floor and the ceiling is suspended from resilient
hangers.

Because so many factors can adversely affect the acoustical performance of a
panel when it is installed in a building, the importance of the inclusion in
building codes of a provision for field testing is readily apparent. The specifica-
tion of certain types of partition construction alone is simply not sufficient to
guarantee the completed construction will provide the desired acoustical privacy.
In particular, the role that poor workmanship plays in the inferior acoustical
performance of finished constructions cannot be overstated.

In Europe, where home ownership has been beyond the grasp of a large
segment of the population and where a long history of apartment or town house
type living has prevailed, many countries have adopted codes for noise insulation
in dwellings that are considerably more stringent than those presently in effect
in the United States and Canada. For example, Germany uses single-figure
ratings derived from reference contours for both airborne and impact sound
insulation. For airborne sound, field or laboratory measurements of sound
transmission loss are made in sixteen one-third octave bands and compared with
the appropriate reference contour in Figure 3-8. An average unfavorable
deviation of 2 dB is permitted. In this computation, favorable deviations are
assumed to lie on the reference contour and are assigned a value of zero. The

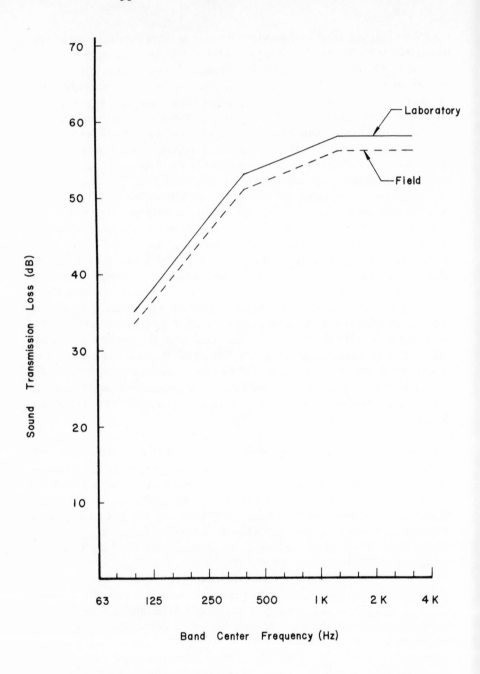

Figure 3-8. Reference Contours for Airborne Sound Insulation Required in Germany. Note: Measurements are made in 1/3-octave bands.[2]

corresponding STC values required by these reference contours are 54 and 52 for laboratory and field measurements respectively.

With a "standard" tapping machine operating on the floor above, impact sound pressure levels are measured in one-third octave bands, normalized to a reference room absorption of 10 m^2, and compared with the reference contour in Figure 3-9. When the average unfavorable deviation has been computed in a manner analogous with that for airborne noise, a single figure rating is obtained. This reference contour would require a floor-ceiling assembly to have an IIC value of 47.

Norway, Denmark, and Czechoslovakia have requirements similar to the German code. Many countries, such as England, the Netherlands, Sweden, and the U.S.S.R., have established different requirements (in the form of reference contours) for different quality classes of dwellings. While a survey of European building codes is somewhat beyond the scope of this work, a summary of such codes can be found in *Airborne, Impact and Structure Borne Noise Control in Multifamily Dwellings.*[2]

In addition to enacting comprehensive building codes, governments could take other steps to reduce noise in homes and apartments. Home appliance and building equipment manufacturers could be required to provide sound power ratings of the products they market. Maximum sound power ratings for certain types of equipment, such as washers, driers, dishwashers, and window air conditioners, could subsequently be incorporated in building codes.

Much more can and desperately needs to be done to control noise from outdoor sources. A number of cities in the United States and Canada as well as some European countries have adopted what are frequently called "noise performance standards." Often these standards are included in the zoning ordinance and they are usually designed to limit noise in commercial or industrial districts which border residential areas. Too often, the limits imposed on industrial districts are so high they fail to provide a satisfactory acoustical environment for neighboring residential areas, and sometimes such ordinances place no restrictions on noise generated within the residential area itself. Stringent noise performance standards along with limitations on the sound power level of equipment such as air conditioners, power lawn mowers, and power leaf rakers could appreciably reduce the noise from such sources.

In the United States, at least, the Noise Control Act of 1972 may lead to noise emission standards for such equipment as well as for home appliances (such as washers, dishwashers, garbage disposals, food blenders, vacuum cleaners, etc.). However, the wording of the legislation would appear to make the establishment of regulatory standards for such equipment and appliances discretionary with the administrator of EPA rather than mandatory (see Chapter 2).

Bylaw No. 846 of the Metropolitan Corporation of Greater Winnipeg is an example of an ordinance designed to limit noise of essentially industrial origin in

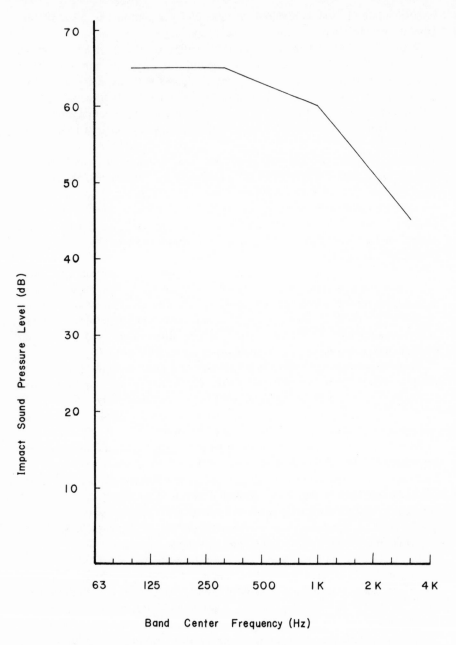

Figure 3-9. Reference Contour for Impact Sound Insulation Required in Germany. Note: Measurements are made in 1/3-octave bands and normalized to a reference room absorption of 10 m^2.

neighboring residential districts. Section 1505.1(c), Maximum Permitted Decibel Levels, provides that:

In the M2-A (Light Industrial) District, the sound pressure level resulting from any activity, whether open or closed, shall not exceed, at any point on or beyond any lotline, the maximum permitted decibel levels for the designated octave band as set forth in the following table. In the enforcement of this regulation, sounds produced by the operation of motor vehicles or other transportation facilities shall not be included in determining the maximum permitted decibel levels.

Maximum Permitted Octave Band Sound Pressure Level
(in decibels)

Octave Band (Hz)	dB
0-75	79
75-150	74
150-300	66
300-600	59
600-1200	53
1200-2400	47
2400-4800	41
Above 4800	39

d) Special Provisions Applying Along District Boundaries. Whenever the "M2-A" District adjoins an "R" Residential District or a "C" Commercial District, at any point at the district boundary, the maximum permitted decibel levels in all octave bands shall be reduced by six decibels from the maximum levels set forth in subsection (c) above.

When the octave band levels in the table above are converted to A-weighting, the maximum allowable noise level in an M-2A District is 62 dB(A). At the boundary of a residential district the maximum permissible level would be 56 dB(A)—a high level indeed for a residential area at night. The city of Winnipeg apparently recognizes this fact and is reported to be considering drafting new legislation.

Edmonton, in 1970, enacted a general anti-noise ordinance (Bylaw No. 3256) which includes certain performance standards. The relevant sections of the code are as follows:

7. A noise level in a residential or in a commercial and industrial area shall be measured at the property line of the property from which the noise is emanating and in the region from which the complaint respecting the noise has been noted.
8. No person shall cause nor permit to be caused a noise level in a residential zone during daytime hours that exceeds 65 dB(A) unless the noise level results from an emergency situation or unless the noise level has been

approved by a special permit issued by the City Commissioners or unless the noise is a temporary and intermittent noise of limited duration as hereinafter permitted.

9. No person shall cause nor permit to be caused in a residential zone during daylight hours a temporary or intermittent noise except to the extent herein set forth:

Time	2 Hours	1 Hour	30 Minutes	15 Minutes
dB(A)	70	75	80	83

The time indicated in the table is the total elapsed time in any calendar day.

10. No person shall cause nor permit to be caused in a residential zone during the night hours any noise that registers more than 50 dB(A), except as otherwise provided under traffic noise control provisions of this bylaw and regulations of the Edmonton Traffic Bylaw and the Edmonton Streets Bylaw.

11. No person shall cause nor permit to be caused in a commercial and industrial zone a noise level in excess of 75 dB(A) except for intermittent noises or those created in an emergency situation or such noises as are permitted temporarily by a special permit issued by the City.

12. In a commercial and industrial zone a person may cause or permit an intermittent noise in accordance with the following table:

Time	2 Hours	1 Hour or Less
dB(A)	80	85

The time indicated in the table is the total elapsed time in any calendar day.

While this ordinance is fairly restrictive, one might well question the provision which allows a 65 dB(A) daytime noise level of unlimited duration at the property line in a residential district. In an area where the daytime ambient level might be 35-45 dB(A), a 65 dB(A) noise level could present a serious intrusion. While it is true that some equipment one might wish to operate would not presently be able to meet substantially lower noise requirements, legislation should foster improved noise control rather than accommodate the existing.

The noise performance standards of Beverly Hills, California, affords an example of a highly restrictive ordinance. Section 4-8.107 states:

It shall be unlawful to operate any machinery, equipment, pump, fan, air-conditioning apparatus or similar mechanical device, in any manner so as to create any noise which would cause the noise level at the adjoining property line to exceed either the limiting noise spectra set forth in the table below, or to exceed the ambient noise level by more than three (3) decibels.

Table of Limiting Noise Levels

Octave Band Center Frequency (Hz)	Band Pressure Level in Decibels
31.5	59
63	58

Table of Limiting Noise Levels (cont.)

Octave Band Center Frequency (Hz)	Band Pressure Level in Decibels
125	49
250	41
500	35
1000	30
2000	28
4000	26
8000	25
16000	24

These octave band levels, when converted to A-weighting, yield a maximum noise level of 40 dB(A).

Control of noise, both indoors and outdoors, in residential areas clearly demands a program and a coordinated approach to the problem from builders, city planners, transportation system designers, and legislators. Furthermore, if significant progress toward this goal is to be realized, responsible individuals in city planning, transportation system design and planning, building departments, and enforcement agencies must be given some training in acoustics and noise control. Inadequate knowledge among public officials is presently one of the greatest impediments to a quiet environment.

4 Construction Noise

Construction noise is often excused as a "temporary nuisance," even though in most large cities it continues day after day, year after year. The large, diesel-powered equipment constitutes the major noise generator at most construction sites. In its 1967 survey of heavy earthmoving equipment, the U.S. Public Health Service found noise levels as high as 120 dB(A) in the operator's compartment of such equipment. Some of the large air compressors that are used to operate jackhammers and pneumatic drills produce nearly 100 dB(A) at a distance of 25 feet, and the jackhammers themselves are almost as noisy.

Although more research and development work is urgently needed on the technical problems associated with construction noise abatement, existing technology is capable of providing substantial relief. Unfortunately, this technology is not being adequately employed, principally because cities have thus far failed to enact ordinances to control construction noise, and in the absence of any regulation, construction companies find the production of noise more profitable than its abatement. New York City, for example, has a basic noise code which exempts daytime construction on weekdays from any noise control requirements. Furthermore, because of a number of loopholes in the code, construction companies can frequently obtain permits for night work. It should be noted, however, that there are some areas in New York City which are almost uninhabited at night and where night work creates a less objectionable nuisance than daytime construction.

In an effort to show what can be done, Citizens for a Quieter City in New York in December of 1967 demonstrated a muffled air compressor developed in Great Britain which reduced the noise level from 86 to 79 dB(A) at a distance of 25 feet. The muffling effect was achieved by a plastic housing lined with foam plastic that enclosed the unit. This organization also demonstrated a muffled jackhammer which produced 82 dB(A) at 25 feet instead of the usual 96. Tests at the British Building Research Station have shown that jackhammer noise can be muffled considerably without any significant impairment of performance. Many European cities are already using muffled jackhammers and air compressors equipped with sound attenuating devices. American manufacturers are just beginning to produce quieter air compressors and muffled jackhammers. The Mayor's Task Force on Noise Control for New York City has recommended that jackhammers and pneumatic drills be surrounded by portable acoustic panels, at least until much quieter equipment or alternative methods are available. Use of bolted steel construction rather than riveted work would eliminate the noisy

57

riveting machines (about 94 dB(A) at 25 feet) used so extensively on high-rise construction. Some of the techniques available for reducing construction noise were illustrated by the Diesel Construction Company in the erection of a 52-story office building in lower Manhattan. Foundation blasting was muffled with special steel wire mesh blankets, demolition was done during late hours and weekends when few people were in the area, and steel beams were welded together than riveted together.

Alleviation of noise from diesel-powered heavy earthmoving equipment presents a somewhat more difficult problem, but even here substantial reductions could be achieved through use of large mufflers on the exhaust. This subject will be treated in more detail in the next chapter.

Thus, even with existing technology, substantial reductions in construction noise are possible for a modest cost. If such reductions are to be realized, however, the public must demand the necessary ordinances from city governments. Furthermore, national governments should immediately commit additional resources to needed research on construction noise abatement.

In the U.S., the Noise Control Act of 1972 may eventually lead to noise emission regulations for construction equipment. Under the terms of this new legislation, the administrator of EPA is empowered to establish noise emission standards for construction equipment, although he is not required to do so (see Chapter 2). It is also important to note that such standards would apply only to new equipment manufactured after the effective date of the standards.

5 Motor Vehicle Noise

The increasing world population and rising levels of economic affluence that have occurred since the Second World War have been accompanied by a staggering increase in the number of motor vehicles. During the twenty-year period 1950-1970 the number of registered motor vehicles in the United States increased at an average annual rate of 4.10 percent, from 49.8 million to 111.2 million. While the number of motor vehicles in Canada is smaller, the 6.10 percent growth rate during this same twenty-year period was nearly 50 percent higher than that for the United States. Canadian registrations increased from 2.60 million to 8.50 million.

Today, every major city from Tokyo to Rome is clogged with cars. Not surprisingly, noise radiation from motor vehicles has become a major source of complaint among urban and suburban dwellers.

Although city residents have traditionally suffered most from motor vehicle noise, the rapid increase in the number of motor vehicles, the production of larger and noisier trucks, the construction of high-speed expressways, and the exodus of people from city to suburb (in no small measure, incidentally, to escape the noise of the city) have increasingly brought noise pollution to suburban areas and the countryside. The pattern has become all too familiar. City dwellers, tired of the noise, dirt, pollution, congestion, and high taxes in the city flee to the solitude of the suburbs. Nearly always, however, they continue to hold jobs in the central city to which they commute by private auto. Their numbers begin to overwhelm the highway system which was originally designed to serve a rural community. The characteristic North American response is to build a bigger highway—a freeway—to link the suburb with other suburban areas and the central city. In the process, of course, the serenity of the suburb is shattered, and it becomes just another city in the spreading megalopolis.

Several surveys have demonstrated just how extensive motor vehicle noise pollution has become. The first really comprehensive citywide survey ever made appears to be the one undertaken in New York City between November of 1929 and May 1930 by the New York Noise Abatement Commission. This commission was formed in the fall of 1929 as a result of mounting citizen complaints over noise, and published the results of its finding in a report, *City Noise*, in 1930. Results from a questionnaire indicated that traffic noise was responsible for 36 percent of the complaints, public transportation for 16 percent, radios (in homes, stores, and streets) for 12 percent, collections and deliveries for 9 percent, whistles and bells for 8 percent, construction for 7.5 percent, and miscellaneous sources for 11.5 percent. The results of that early survey are especially significant when viewed in the light of more recent findings. The data in *City Noise*, obtained from measurements at 97 different locations, suggest the noise level in New York City ranged from 50 to 78 dB(A) and averaged about 70 dB(A). In a recent survey made in New York City, the noise level ranged from 61 to 84 dB(A) and averaged about 68 dB(A). What is somewhat surprising, however, is a survey taken in downtown Philadelphia about this same time in which the average noise level was 69 dB(A) with a range from 62 to 83 dB(A). The results of these surveys suggest that the noise level in New York City is not changing appreciably while conditions in other major cities are rapidly approaching those in New York—a rather unpleasant prospect to contemplate.[1]

One of the most comprehensive noise surveys ever made was the London survey in 1961. Noise measurements were made at 540 locations in central London, and 1,400 residents at those locations were interviewed. The measurements showed that traffic noise predominated at 84 percent of the points, and about one-third of the people interviewed specifically mentioned motor vehicle noise as a major irritant. Equally significant is the fact that comparison of these results with the results of an earlier survey showed that the percentage of people disturbed by noise that arose outside the home increased from 23 percent in 1948 to 50 percent in 1961.[2]

The effect of motor vehicle traffic on urban noise levels is well illustrated by the results of a noise survey conducted in Tokyo during 1965 and 1966. The city is zoned for residential, commercial, limited industrial, and industrial uses. A time distribution of noise in the city was obtained by measurement of the sound level at one point in each zone once an hour for a 24-hour period. At each point a traffic count was also made. In Figure 5-1 median noise levels in a residential zone are shown as a function of time of day. Traffic density is also shown. We see that there is a high correlation between traffic density and the measured noise levels. One must recognize, of course, that traffic outside the immediate vicinity of the measuring location contributes to the measured noise levels in such surveys. For example, between midnight and 2 A.M. there was a further decline in the noise level even though the traffic count was unchanged. Nevertheless, the traffic count gives some indication of the amount of motor vehicle traffic throughout the city.[3,4]

The variation of noise level with time in an industrial area is quite different from that for the residential area (see Figure 5-2). While traffic substantially increases the noise level in the industrial area, the nighttime noise level remains very much above the level in a residential area. Thus, most of the noise in this residential area is clearly due to motor vehicle traffic—a situation common to most large cities today. Indeed, the New York Mayor's Task Force, in its report, *Toward A Quieter City*, observes: "The Task Force finds that vehicular traffic, especially truck traffic is the single constant source of pervasive noise in the city."[5]

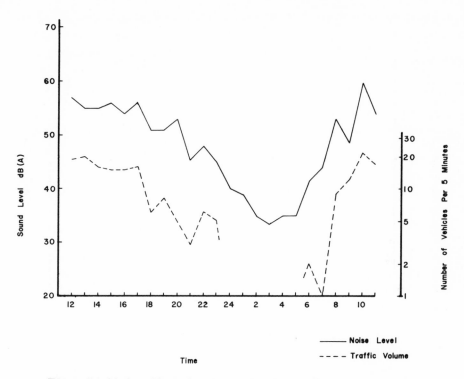

Figure 5-1. Median Noise Level in a Residential Zone in Tokyo as a Function of Time of Day.[3]

A number of studies have shown that the noise problem near high-speed highways arises principally from trucks, motorcycles, and sports cars. In a series of tests conducted along California highways in 1964, the California Highway Patrol measured the noise levels of 25,351 passenger cars, 4,656 gasoline trucks, and 5,838 diesel trucks. Tests were conducted at a number of representative locations throughout the state with a sound level meter, equipped with an A-weighting network, located 25 feet from the center of the right-hand traffic lane 12 feet in width. Observations were perforce limited to the outside lanes of the highway. Trucks and slow passenger cars tend to travel in the outside lanes while faster passenger vehicles, sports cars, and motorcycles are frequently in the inner lanes. Hence the truck sample is probably a representative one while the noise levels obtained on passenger cars are probably somewhat low. Noise levels for the passenger cars varied between 71 and 92 dB(A), the average being about 82 dB(A). Noise levels for the diesel trucks, however, ranged between 74 and 105 dB(A) with the average being about 93 dB(A).[6]

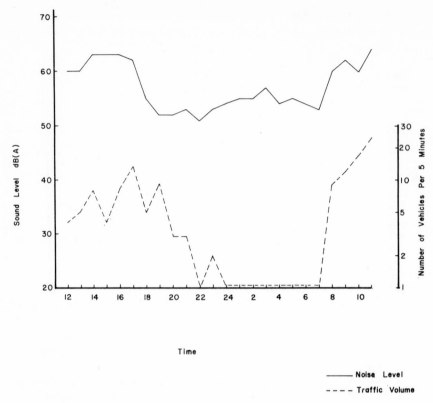

Figure 5-2. Median Noise Level in an Industrial Zone in Tokyo as a Function of Time of Day.[3]

Results of these various surveys show quite clearly that if quieter living conditions are to be realized, cities must reduce motor vehicle noise. Yet, with a few noteworthy exceptions, governments at all levels have generally failed to achieve any significant reductions.

In the United States, control of motor vehicle noise generally is vested in the state government, and nearly all states have motor vehicle codes which require, among other things, that a motor vehicle be equipped with an adequate muffler. Indiana's code is fairly typical. Section 47-2230(a) states:

Every motor vehicle shall at all times be equipped with a muffler in good working order and in constant operation to prevent excessive or unusual noise or annoying smoke, and no person shall use a muffler cutout, by-pass or similar device upon a motor vehicle operated on a street or highway.

Similarly in most Canadian provinces, control of motor vehicle noise is vested in the provincial government (Labrador, Manitoba, New Brunswick, Newfoundland, Nova Scotia, Prince Edward Island). All of these provinces have codes similar to the Indiana statute. Regulation 12 of Newfoundland's 1970 Highway Traffic Regulations is fairly typical. It specifies:

No person shall operate upon any highway a motor vehicle not equipped with a muffler in good working order and preventing excessive or unusual noise from the exhaust, and no muffler cutout shall be installed upon any motor vehicle.

The chief difficulty with all such codes is that they fail to spell out in quantitative terms the noise levels at which violations would occur. That part of the law dealing with altered exhaust systems is relatively easy to enforce, but terms such as "excessive or unusual noise," "adequate muffler," "muffler in good working order" are not defined nor are they subject to easy or precise definition. One can today buy a wide variety of replacement mufflers that emit much higher noise levels than the original equipment but which would still satisfy the requirements of such codes. Furthermore, original equipment mufflers on most new motorcycles allow much higher noise levels than necessary. United States courts have held, however, that in the absence of quantitatively defined noise limits for motor vehicles, original equipment mufflers meet the criteria of "adequate" and "muffler in good working order." Deteriorating mufflers, particularly on trucks, present another difficult enforcement problem. Truck mufflers deteriorate with age. In the absence of quantitative standards, however, demonstrating that such a muffler produces a higher noise level than the original equipment or that such noise is "excessive or unusual" is, at best, difficult. Because of such enforcement problems, statutes such as these are seldom effectively enforced. Manitoba has enacted enabling legislation which authorizes the Provincial Department of Highways to prescribe motor vehicle noise standards measured in decibels, and the Department is studying possible regulations under this authority.

At the present time, in Alberta, British Columbia, Ontario, Quebec, and Saskatchewan there exists a sort of joint authority between the provincial government and the cities for control of motor vehicle noise. The motor vehicle statutes in all five provinces require that a motor vehicle be equipped with a muffler. In addition, some cities in these provinces have enacted bylaws to control motor vehicle noise. Most such bylaws are subjective in nature, utilizing terms such as objectionable, loud, and excessive. For example, in 1967 the City of Vancouver enacted the following bylaw (No. 4338):

1. This by-law may be cited as the "Motor Vehicle Noise Abatement By-law."
2. The following noises are, in the opinion of the Council of the City of Vancouver, objectionable noises:
    i. The squeal of a tire on a road surface emitted by a motor vehicle which is accelerating;
    ii. The squeal of a tire on a road surface emitted by a motor vehicle during a change in the course of direction of travel of the motor vehicle;

iii. Any loud, roaring or explosive sound emitted by a motor vehicle.
3. The following terms, whenever used in this by-law, shall have the meanings respectively ascribed to them in this section:
   i. "Motor Vehicle" means a vehicle, not run upon rails, that is designed to be self-propelled;
   ii. "Road surface" means gravel, asphalt, cement or material of any kind whatsoever placed upon any road, highway, bridge, viaduct, lane, or any way designed or intended for use by the general public for the passage of vehicles and every private place or passageway to which the public, for the purpose of the parking or servicing of vehicles, has access or is invited.
4. No person shall make or cause to be made any objectionable noise set forth in Section 2 hereof.
5. No person shall operate a motor vehicle so as to cause a nuisance by noise therefrom.
6. Every person who offends against any of the provisions of this by-law, or who suffers or permits any act or thing to be done in contravention or in violation of any of the provisions of this by-law, or who does any act or thing which violates any of the provisions of this by-law, shall be deemed to be guilty of an offense against this by-law, and shall be liable to the penalties hereinafter imposed.
7. (1) Every person who commits an offense against Section 4 of this by-law is liable to a fine and penalty not exceeding one hundred ($100.00) dollars and costs, or in default of payment thereof or in the alternative, to imprisonment with or without hard labour for any period not exceeding two months;
   (2) Every person who commits an offense against Section 5 of this by-law is liable to a fine and penalty of not less than fifty ($50.00) dollars and not exceeding one hundred ($100.00) dollars and costs, or in default of payment thereof or in the alternative, to imprisonment with or without hard labor for any period not exceeding two months.
8. It is thereby declared that this by-law is passed with the intention that Sections 4 and 5 shall be independent of each other so that should either of the said sections be declared invalid then the section declared invalid shall be severable from the by-law.
9. The provisions of this by-law are in addition to, not in substitution for, the provisions of By-law No. 2531 as amended, being a by-law for the abatement and control of noise in the City of Vancouver.
10. This by-law shall come into force and take effect on and after the date of the final passing hereof.

DONE AND PASSED in Open Council this 28th day of November, 1967.

Because of the obvious lack of objectivity, Vancouver has appointed a committee to investigate noise pollution and recommend appropriate control measures.

Both the City of Ottawa and the Municipality of Metropolitan Toronto have enacted bylaws which set maximum allowable noise limits, measured in dB, for motor vehicles. Such bylaws will be discussed shortly.

In the province of Alberta, the two major cities, Edmonton and Calgary, have enacted bylaws similar to the one adopted by the Municipality of Metropolitan Toronto. Also, the Provincial government recently established a Department of the Environment which is reportedly considering possible noise legislation for the Province.

In 1965 New York became the first state in the United States to set a quantitatively defined limit on motor vehicle noise. Section 386 of the New York Vehicle and Traffic Law contains the following provisions:

1. No motor vehicle, other than an authorized emergency vehicle or a vehicle moving under special permit, which makes or creates excessive or unusual noise shall operate upon a public highway.
2. A motor vehicle which produces a sound level of 88 decibels or more on the "A" scale shall be deemed to make or create excessive or unusual noise.
    a. Sound pressure levels in decibels shall be measured on the "A" scale of a standard sound level meter having characteristics defined by American Standard Association Specification S 1.4–1961 "General Purpose Sound Level Meter." Measurements of sound pressure level shall be made in accordance with applicable measurement practices outlined in the Society of Automotive Engineers Standard J672 "Measurement of Truck and Bus Noise" as approved January, 1957. The microphone shall be placed at a distance of 50 feet plus or minus 2 feet from the center of the lane in which the vehicle is traveling.
    b. Measurements of sound pressure level shall be made at speeds of less than 35 miles per hour.
    c. No arrest shall be made in cases where the noise limit is exceeded by less than a 2 decibel tolerance.

Reduction of truck noise along expressways in residential areas of Westchester County seems to have been the principal objective of the law. The statute has been extensively enforced only in Westchester County in areas near toll stations on the Thomas E. Dewey Thruway where traffic is moving slowly.[7] In its report, *Toward a Quieter City*, the New York Mayor's Task Force on Noise Control makes the following observations on the New York statute:

The Task Force is convinced that the State's open highway regulation permitting trucks to operate at a noise level of 88 dB(A)–measured at 50 feet from the center of the lane in which the truck is traveling and based on a speed of 35 m.p.h.–is completely unrealistic for conditions in the city. This law was intended to control noise on the open highway and not in the city where the building lines of many streets are only 60 feet apart, meaning that the permissible noise level of the sidewalks of New York under the State statute is well above the hearing conservation criterion.

In the event that the state law is not amended to meet the needs of the State's urban population, New York City should promulgate its own standards in an ordinance or regulation to limit the noise of motor vehicles. While working to obtain corrective state legislation, or to develop a City regulation, which might require permission from the State legislature, sometimes a long and arduous process, the City should seriously consider routing truck traffic away from noise sensitive areas.[5]

In 1967, the California Legislature added Sections 23130 and 27160 to the Vehicle Code. Section 27160 states that no person shall sell or offer for sale a new motor vehicle which produces a noise level exceeding specified limits at a distance of 50 feet from the centerline of travel under the test procedures. For vehicles manufactured after January 1, 1973, these limits are 86 dB(A) for heavy trucks and motorcycles, and 84 dB(A) for all other motor vehicles. The test procedure used is one developed by the Society of Automotive Engineers Acoustical Committee: SAE J366, Exterior Sound Level for Heavy Trucks and Buses.[8],[9]

Section 23130 establishes maximum permissible noise limits for motor vehicles operating on the highway in two different speed zones.

23130. (a) No person shall operate either a motor vehicle or combination of vehicles of a type subject to registration at any time or under any condition of grade, load, acceleration or deceleration in such a manner as to exceed the following noise limit for the category of motor vehicle based on a distance of 50 feet from the center of the lane of travel within the speed limits specified in this section:

	Speed limit of 35 mph or less	Speed limit of more than 35 mph
(1) Any motor vehicle with a manufacturer's gross vehicle weight rating of 6,000 pounds or more, any combination of vehicles towed by such motor vehicle, and any motorcycle other than a motor-driven cycle	88 dB(A)	92 dB(A)
(2) Any other motor vehicle and any combination of vehicles towed by such motor vehicle	82 dB(A)	86 dB(A)

(b) The department shall adopt regulations establishing the test procedures and instrumentation to be utilized.
(c) This section applies to the total noise from a vehicle or combination of vehicles and shall not be construed as limiting or precluding the enforcement of any other provisions of this code relating to motor vehicle exhaust noise.
(d) For the purpose of this section, a motor truck, truck tractor, or bus that is not equipped with an identification plate or marking bearing the manufacturer's name and manufacturer's gross vehicle weight rating shall be considered as having a manufacturer's gross vehicle weight rating of 6,000 pounds or more if the unladen weight is more than 5,000 pounds.
(e) No person shall have a cause of action relating to the provisions of this section against a manufacturer of a vehicle or a component part thereof on a theory based upon breach of express or implied warranty unless it is alleged and proved that such manufacturer did not comply with noise limit standards of the Vehicle Code applicable to manufacturers and in effect at the time such vehicle or component part was first sold for purposes other than resale.

That these limits are much too high is suggested by the fact that an acoustical consulting firm hired by the state to study motor vehicle noise and its control recommended maximum limits of 87 dB(A) for motorcycles and trucks and 77 dB(A) for all other vehicles. The firm considered these recommended limits to be easily attainable with existing technology, and indeed, they correspond to the average noise levels reported in the 1964 California Highway Patrol study. Measurements in that 1964 study were made at a distance of 25 feet from the center of the traffic lane, while the noise limits set by the 1967 statute are based on a 50-foot distance. In Figure 5-3 the measured noise levels from the California Highway Patrol study have been reduced by 6 dB(A) to correspond to the levels that would have been measured if the meter had been located at the 50-foot distance. A direct comparison can therefore be made between the data in Figure 5-3 and the California noise code.

Comparing the results of that study with the limits established by the 1967

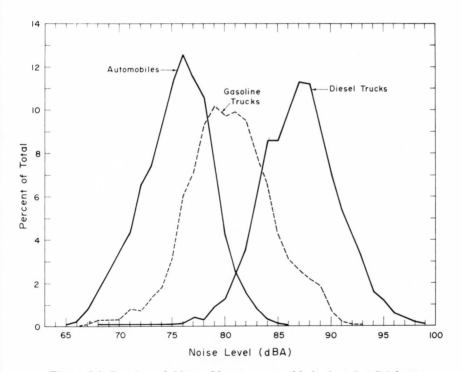

Figure 5-3. Results of Noise Measurements Made by the California Highway Patrol on 25,351 Passenger Cars, 4,656 Gasoline-Powered Trucks, and 5,838 Diesel Trucks. Note: The measured noise levels were reduced by 6 dB so that the levels shown in the figure correspond to the levels that would have been measured at a distance of 50 feet.[6]

noise law, one can readily see that the law should prove completely ineffective against cars and should effectively control the noise level on only a small percentage of diesel trucks. Recent data from the California Highway Patrol bear out this conclusion. In a little more than a year after that agency began enforcing the new law early in 1969, nearly 606,000 vehicles were monitored. Only 2,861 or about 0.5 percent were found to be in violation of the law, and nearly all of these were trucks. In the Sacramento area, for example, of 97,746 vehicles measured, 658 were in violation of the law, and 630 of these were trucks.

As a result of this experience the California Legislature in 1970 lowered the allowable noise limits for motor vehicles. The 1970 amendment to Section 23130 of the Vehicle Code sets the following noise limits:

	Speed limit of 35 mph or less	Speed limit of more than 35 mph
(1) Any motor vehicle with a manufacturer's gross vehicle weight rating of 6000 pounds or more and any combination of vehicles towed by such motor vehicle:		
(A) Before January 1, 1973 . . .	88 dB(A)	90 dB(A)
(B) On and after January 1, 1973	86 dB(A)	90 dB(A)
(2) Any motorcycle other than a motor-driven cycle	82 dB(A)	86 dB(A)
(3) Any other motor vehicle and any combination of vehicles towed by such motor vehicle . . .	76 dB(A)	82 dB(A)

This amended code sets significantly lower allowable noise levels for passenger cars and motorcycles but the 2 dB reduction in limits for truck noise will be of little consequence. Even so, no sound argument has been advanced to justify higher noise limits for motorcycles than for passenger cars. There is certainly no technical reason why a 50 hp motorcycle should be allowed to make as much noise as four 300 hp Cadillacs, yet even the amended code permits precisely this situation.

The lower limits established by this amended code resulted in a greater number of violations reported the following year. During 1971, the California Highway Patrol found 8,157 vehicles in violation of Section 23130. Yet, these violations comprised only about 1.4 percent of the heavy trucks, 8.5 percent of the motorcycles, and 0.4 percent of the passenger cars monitored during that year. Furthermore, nearly one-third of the heavy trucks in violation of the code had defective exhaust systems and over one-half of the motorcycles had modified exhaust systems designed to increase the noise level.[9]

Unfortunately, because of lack of enforcement, the California statutes have not been very effective in controlling motor vehicle noise, particularly in urban areas. Lack of effective enforcement apparently stems principally from apathy on the part of public officials rather than from any technical difficulties in measuring noise levels or obtaining compliance. The State Highway Patrol is essentially the only agency in the state that attempted to enforce even the 1967 law, and because of fund limitations, it had equipped only six teams with sound measuring equipment to cover the entire state four years after enactment of the statute. In January of 1971 there were more than 14.2 million motor vehicles registered in California. If a million vehicles are monitored each year, the probability of a vehicle being checked in any given year is only one in fourteen.

Only a very few local governments in California are known to have sound level meters in use. Part of the difficulty for municipalities stems from the restrictions established by the state for measuring sites. These restrictions specify that a site used for measuring noise from vehicles under Section 23130 must be an open area free of large reflecting surfaces such as parked vehicles, building, signboards, hills, or trees within a 100-foot radius of the microphone and within a 100-foot radius of the point on the centerline of the path of the vehicle when it is opposite the microphone (see Figure 5-4). Furthermore, this area must be free from standing water, shrubs, or grass over 6 inches high. These restrictions, which are taken from the Society of Automotive Engineers New Vehicle Test Procedure, effectively preclude measurement in most residential and commercial zones of cities. Nevertheless, in unincorporated areas, appropriate measuring sites do exist, and local governments do have enforcement tools at their disposal which they have not effectively utilized.[8,9]

In recent years, motorcycles have become an increasingly irritating source of noise. Between 1960 and 1970, United States motorcycle registrations increased at an average annual rate of 17 percent from 570,000 to 2,781,000. In California, which accounted for 20 percent of the motorcycle registrations in 1970, our own surveys indicate that probably one-fifth of the motorcycles have modified exhaust systems installed for the purpose of amplifying exhaust noise, despite a provision in the vehicle code which prohibits such modifications. Enforcement agencies not equipped with sound monitoring equipment clearly have authority to apprehend the operators of such vehicles but are apparently unwilling to do so. In Berkeley, for example, where 26 percent of the motorcycles in our sample had modified exhaust systems, only one such citation has been issued in the past two years.

The Federal Noise Control Act of 1972, although directed primarily at noise reduction in new products (see Chapter 2), does contain a provision which requires the administrator of the Environmental Protection Agency to establish noise emission standards for trucks and buses engaged in interstate commerce that are already on the road. Of considerable importance is the fact that this provision also contains a federal preemption clause which prohibits a state or local government from establishing or enforcing a noise limit different from the

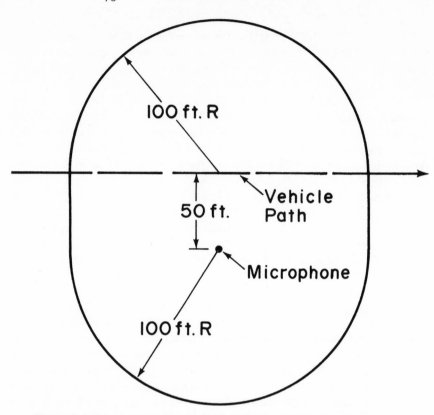

Figure 5-4. Restrictions Established by the State of California for Vehicle Noise Measuring Sites. Note: The California State Administrative Code requires that any location used for measuring noise from vehicles on the highway under Section 23130 of the State Vehicle Code must be free of large reflecting surfaces such as buildings, parked vehicles, signboards, hillsides, or trees, within an area surrounding the measuring site as shown here.

federal one after a federal standard has been promulgated. Once federal standards are implemented, California will no longer be able to enforce that part of Section 23130 of the State Vehicle Code which deals with truck noise. While the desirability of uniform federal standards for *new* vehicles is understandable from the manufacturer's viewpoint, the case for federal preemption of noise emission regulations for the operation of vehicles already on the road has not been made.[10]

Turning our attention next to the situation in Canada, we find that none of the provincial governments have as yet set maximum allowable noise limits for motor vehicles, although such legislation is reported to be under consideration in Alberta, British Columbia, and Manitoba.

Several cities, however, have adopted bylaws which spell out maximum permissible noise levels in decibels. In 1958 the Municipality of Metropolitan Toronto enacted Bylaw 835. This bylaw, as amended in 1962, states:

The Council of the Municipality of Metropolitan Toronto HEREBY ENACTS as follows:

1. In this by-law,
    (a) "motor vehicle" means automobile, motorcycle and any other vehicle propelled or driven otherwise than by muscular power and used for the transportation of persons or things but does not include the cars of electric or steam railways or other motor vehicles running only upon rails.
    (b) "Undue noise" means any sound, the overall sound pressure level of which exceeds 94 decibels when measured at a distance of 15 feet or more from its source by use of the C-weighting scale and the "slow" setting of a sound-level meter.
    (c) "Sound-level meter" means an instrument consisting of the following components:
        (i) Meter type 1551-A manufactured by the General Radio Company of Cambridge, Massachusetts, U.S.A., without a Rochelle-salt-crystal diaphragm type microphone.
        (ii) Microphone transformer type No. 759-P26 manufactured by the General Radio Company of Cambridge, Massachusetts, U.S.A.
        (iii) Dynamic microphone type 759-P27 manufactured by the General Radio Company of Cambridge, Massachusetts, U.S.A. or its equivalent type No. 633-A dynamic microphone as manufactured by either the Northern Electric Company of Canada Limited or the Altec Lansing Corporation, California, U.S.A.
        (iv) Microphone extension cables type No. 759-P22 as manufactured by the General Radio Company of Cambridge, Massachusetts, U.S.A. which when appropriately assembled provides a means of measurement of noise and other sounds in decibels when acoustically calibrated at a frequency of 1,000 cycles per second to measure the overall sound pressure level at the microphone thereof relative to 0.0002 microbars.
2. No person shall drive or operate any motor vehicle that creates an undue noise within the limits of The Municipality of Metropolitan Toronto.
3. The provisions of this By-law shall not apply to the operation of police, fire department or ambulance sirens, horns or bells in the course of duty or vital necessity.
4. Every person who contravenes any of the provisions of this by-law shall upon conviction thereof, forfeit and pay, at the discretion of the convicting magistrate a penalty not exceeding (exclusive of costs) $300.00 for each offence.
5. This By-law shall not become operative until approved by the Department of Transport.

ENACTED AND PASSED this 21st day of October, A.D. 1958.

The metropolitan government has evidently experienced enforcement difficulties. In a letter dated May 27, 1969, to the Honolulu, Hawaii Mayor's Noise Control Committee, the Metropolitan Solicitor makes the following comments on Bylaw 835:

In 1964 a prosecution was brought under this by-law and the matter went ultimately to the Ontario Court of Appeal, where both the conviction and the validity of the by-law were upheld. The evidence necessary to obtain the conviction was of a technical nature, requiring proof of the accuracy of the sound level meter. The case went on for two or three days and necessitated the employment of expert witnesses . . .

The Metropolitan Toronto Police have concluded that the difficulties involved in the use of the sound level meter outweigh its usefulness and for several years now no prosecutions have been launched under By-law 835, the Police acting instead under Section 42 of the Ontario Highway Traffic Act with regard to motor vehicle noise . . .

Generally speaking, the experience here has been that enactments which provide what may be termed a human standard, i.e., which prohibit "unnecessary," "unreasonable," or "undue" noise are more workable than the one involving the mechanical standard. It should however be borne in mind that the mechnical equipment available today to measure noise may be more sophisticated than that which was in use at the time of passage of By-law 835 . . .

In 1969 the City of Quebec adopted Bylaw No. 1752 to control motor vehicle noise. Section 3 of this bylaw prohibits nuisance from motor vehicles:

3. Are declared nuisances and are prohibited within the limits of the City of Quebec;
    (a) all noise produced by an automobile and exceeding for each category of automobile, the values indicated in Section 6;
    (b) for motorcycles to be operated in groups of more than two at a distance of less than 1500 feet between each group;
    (c) the noise produced by ineffective mufflers or faulty exhaust equipment;
    (d) any excessive or unusual noise likely to disturb the peace, well-being, comfort, tranquility or rest of persons in the neighborhood, produced by the acceleration of an automobile at an excessive speed, or by excessively racing an automobile engine, either in starting or while stationary, or produced by repeated acceleration;
    (e) noise produced by unnecessary or abusive use of an automobile horn or siren (klaxon);
    (f) all excessive or unusual noise likely to disturb the peace, well-being, comfort, tranquility or rest of persons in the neighborhood, caused by the gathering of automobiles anywhere in the City;
    (g) all excessive or unusual noise produced by a radio or other instrument designed to reproduce sound in an automobile . . .

Section 4 prohibits the operation of motorcycles in the streets or lanes of Old Quebec and in certain other specified streets of the City.

Section 6 establishes the maximum permissible noise limits for motor vehicles in decibels:

6. Noise produced by an automobile must not exceed, for vehicles of the category indicated, the volume shown in the following table, these volumes being subject to a tolerance of one decibel:

Categories of Vehicles	Sound Level Maxima in Decibels
(a) Motorcycles	86
(b) Pleasure vehicles, taxis	83
(c) Farm vehicles, service vehicles, commercial vehicles, delivery vehicles, and other motor vehicles whose weight when loaded is less than or equal to two tons	83
with loaded weight exceeding two tons	90
(d) Autobus	90

These sound levels are overall sound pressure levels, not dB(A). Since a substantial part of motor vehicle noise is low-frequency noise, dB(A) values corresponding to these limits would be 10-15 dB less.

Unlike most such statutes, this law provides that every peace officer may demand "that every operator or owner of an automobile, have the sound intensity produced by the automobile measured while in his possession, if the noise produced by said automobile seems to, in the opinion of the peace officer or constable, exceed the ratings established by Section 6 of the present By-law." The bylaw also specifies the test conditions. The microphone is to be placed three feet above the ground and at a distance of twenty-five feet from the moving axle of the vehicle. Measurements are made while the vehicle is under full acceleration from a speed of 35 mph.

The City Manager of Quebec states, "The City recently purchased a sound level meter and recorder which we fully intend to use to enforce thoroughly our By-law ... "

This bylaw will probably be effective in the City of Quebec. In a state like California, however, where truck traffic, which is heavily interstate in nature, is a major offender, the test procedures embodied in this law would present an enforcement problem.

In Alberta, where the provincial government has enacted enabling legislation which allows cities to regulate motor vehicle noise, both Edmonton and Calgary have adopted bylaws which set quantitative limits on motor vehicle noise. Sections 4, 5, and 6 of By-Law No. 3256 adopted by the City of Edmonton in 1970 provide that:

4. No person shall operate or cause to be operated a passenger vehicle or truck that has a gross weight of less than 6,000 pounds, the noise from which vehicle measured at a distance of not less than 15 feet from the traffic lane in

which the vehicle is standing or moving has a level greater than 83 dB(A), except for the operation of a "signalling device."

5. No person shall operate or cause to be operated a motorcycle, the noise from which motorcycle measured at a distance of not less than 15 feet from the traffic lane in which the motorcycle is moving or standing has a level greater than 88 dB(A) in the daytime and 83 dB(A) at night, except for the operation of a "signalling device."

6. (1) No person shall operate or cause to be operated a passenger vehicle or truck with rated gross vehicle weight of 6,000 pounds or more, the noise from which truck or passenger vehicle measured at a distance of not less than 15 feet from the traffic lane in which such vehicle is standing or moving has a level greater than 90 dB(A), except for the operation of a "signalling device." (2) When heavy equipment is being used by the City or its agents to build roads or to grade or to sweep and clean roads or to remove snow therefrom then a noise level not exceeding 90 dB(A) will be permissible, providing the noise is only of such duration as is reasonably necessary to improve the highway condition.

Calgary enacted Bylaw No. 7902 in 1970, which establishes the following noise limits, measured at a distance of not less than 15 feet, for the different classes of motor vehicles in different speed zones:

Vehicle Class	Lawful Speed Limit (in miles per hour)	Maximum Noise Intensity dB(A)
Light Motor Vehicle (Passenger vehicle, light motor truck, motorcycle, motor scooter)	not more than 30	80
	more than 30 and not more than 45	85
	more than 45	88
Motor trucks	not more than 30	87
	more than 30 and not more than 45	91
	more than 45	95
Tractor Trailers and Concrete Mixers	not more than 30	88
	more than 30 and not more than 45	94
	more than 45	98

As we have seen, the magnitude of the motor vehicle noise problem has reached such a dimension that a major worldwide abatement program is needed. The future of our cities depends in no small measure on how successful we are in reducing traffic noise and congestion. Three broad approaches are open to us. We can: (1) reduce the noise radiated by the source itself, (2) reduce the noise levels in communities near expressways by use of certain design features and by choice of location, or (3) eliminate the source through substitution of alternate modes of transportation.

Tests by the California Division of Highways have shown that while a diesel truck produces an 80 dB(A) noise level 100 feet from an expressway on flat, open terrain, the noise level at the same distance is reduced to 69 dB(A) if the roadway is depressed 20 feet below the adjacent land. A further reduction to 65 dB(A) is achieved by construction of an 8-foot high noise shield along the right-of-way above the depressed roadway. Trees and shrubs planted along a roadway can greatly enhance the aesthetic appearance of the road and simultaneously provide visual screening of the highway for nearby residents. Trees and shrubs alone, however, do not provide an effective noise shield.[11]

While such design features, coupled with appropriate location of the route, could greatly reduce the noise nuisance in communities near expressways, significant reductions in motor vehicle noise in existing cities can only be achieved through quieting or eliminating the source.

Although the exhaust is the predominant source of noise from an unmuffled motor vehicle, the engine structure, transmission, tires, and vibrations of the outer surface of the vehicle all contribute to the total noise. (These vibrations of the outer surfaces of the vehicle are caused either by direct transmission of road or engine-excited vibrations or by airborne noise from the engine structure which produces vibrations in the vehicle surfaces.) The diesel engine has gradually replaced the gasoline engine in heavy trucks, chiefly because it is more efficient under partial load than the gasoline engine and operates on a cheaper fuel. Because diesel engines operate at considerably higher peak cylinder pressures and rates of pressure rise, they generally produce higher noise and vibration levels than do gasoline engines. During the past twenty years, the noise level of diesel engines in commercial vehicles has increased by about 10 dB(A). While the exhaust is the major source of noise, airborne noise from diesel engines can be a serious problem. As demonstrated by the spectra in Figure 5-5 for a small (2-liter) diesel engine, exhaust noise predominates by about 10 dB over the entire frequency spectrum. Silencing of the engine inlet gives a substantial noise reduction in the frequency range below about 1,000 Hz (curves *B* and *C*). Airborne noise from the engine structure itself is responsible for the remainder of the noise (curve *C*). Correction of these spectra to A-weighting shows the great necessity for reduction of airborne engine noise. The A-weighted sound level for spectrum *A* is 99 dB(A). Complete silencing of the exhaust gives a reduction of 11 dB(A), and silencing of the engine inlet yields a further reduction of only 1 dB(A). The A-weighted level for spectrum *C* is 87 dB(A).[12,13,14]

The level of exhaust noise is determined by many factors, several of which depend on engine design. Through modification of the engine design, the British Internal Combustion Research Institute has successfully reduced the overall level of exhaust noise by some 10-15 dB. The A-weighted level of exhaust noise is also a function of engine speed and increases at a rate of about 45 dB(A) per tenfold increase in engine speed. This rate of increase is essentially independent of the type of exhaust system or silencer used.

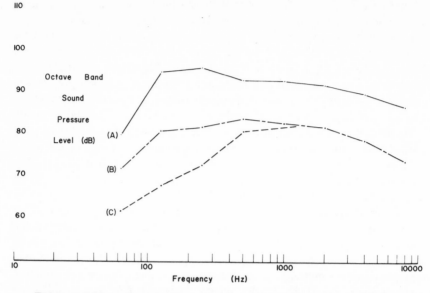

Figure 5-5. Noise Spectra for a Two-Liter Diesel Engine at 1,500 Rpm Under Full Load. Note: Curve *A*, open exhaust and inlet; Curve *B*, silenced exhaust but open inlet; Curve *C*, silenced exhaust and inlet.[14]

Noise produced by the engine structure is somewhat more difficult to control through engine design. One approach has been to build an acoustically lined enclosure around the engine—a technique which reduced the noise level 15-20 dB(A) in tests conducted in Germany. Basically, all that is required is a sealed engine compartment that is mechanically ventilated by a fan and lined with an acoustically absorbent material. Similar designs are already employed on some diesel buses. A modification of this technique should be applicable to motorcycles. Although exhaust noise frequently predominates in the noise emitted by motorcycles, this is amenable to reduction either by more efficient muffler systems or through modifications in engine design. Enclosure of the engine in an acoustically lined housing would greatly reduce airborne engine noise, the next most important source of motorcycle noise. Finally, while little attention has thus far been paid to reduction of engine noise through design modifications, experimental engine designs developed in Britain show considerable promise of yielding 10-15 dB(A) lower noise levels than conventional engines.[14,15,16]

Tire whine is sometimes a significant component of the noise from trucks traveling at high speeds and is the result of certain types of tread design. Some tread designs have vacuum-cup type noise sources either originally or as the tire wears. The aggressive cross-bar tread, for example, is not particularly noisy when new, but wear creates vacuum cups which produce a high frequency whine at high speeds. In the absence of noise performance standards, however, there is little incentive for the tire manufacturers to market anything but an economical, long-life tire.

In the near future, then, noise reductions of 10-15 dB(A) for nearly all types of motor vehicles should be possible for a very modest cost, and even greater reductions should be attainable for particularly noisy vehicles in which exhaust noise predominates.

There are really two aspects, then to the problem of motor vehicle noise control. One is the control of noise from vehicles already on the road by means of existing technology. Nearly all of the recently-enacted state or provincial statutes and local ordinances which specify maximum allowable noise limits for motor vehicles are directed at this aspect of the problem.

The other aspect of the problem is that of forcing the manufacturers to produce quieter vehicles. Our experience with the auto industry and efforts to improve air quality indicates that substantially quieter vehicles will not be forthcoming unless an informed public demands them through appropriate legislation. Clearly, this legislation *must* embody quantitative standards measured in decibels. Qualitative or subjective criteria will prove inadequate, in part because they do not provide the vehicle designer with a quantity which he can measure. National, state, or provincial governments should begin at once the task of setting lower allowable noise limits for new vehicles entering production—an approach widely used today to reduce air pollutant emissions from automobiles. Also governments could effectively use their purchasing power to encourage designs that reduce noise.

In passing the Noise Control Act of 1972 (Public Law 92-574), the U.S. Congress clearly intends for the Environmental Protection Agency to designate motor vehicles as a major source of noise and to establish by regulation noise emission standards for new motor vehicles. Two provisions of this law should be clearly noted, however. One is that, in establishing noise emission standards, EPA is directed to take into account not only the magnitude of the existing noise problem and the reductions achievable through application of the best available technology, but also the cost of compliance. Unless, therefore, the public participates in the rule-making process and demands the reductions which are technologically possible, we can expect vehicle manufacturers to use the cost argument to lobby against noise standards as they have done with air quality standards. Secondly, since the Noise Control Act contains a federal preemption clause, after the effective date of a federal standard, no state or local government may establish or enforce a different standard (see Chapter 2). Once federal standards become effective, California can no longer enforce Section 27160 of its Vehicle Code. The objective of federal preemption in tbe establishment of these standards essentially is to provide a single standard with which manufacturers must comply rather than a multitude of different ones. How effective this approach will be in reducing noise levels remains to be seen.[10]

Canada has also established noise standards for new motor vehicles. Under the Motor Vehicle Safety Act, the Canadian Ministry of Transport amended Schedule C of the Federal Motor Vehicle Safety Regulations to include noise standards for buses, motorcycles, minibikes, passenger cars, and multipurpose passenger vehicles. These regulations, which were published as SOR/72-248 in the *Canada Gazette, Part II* on July 26, 1972, add Section 1106, which states:

1106. Every vehicle shall be so constructed that
  (a) it complies with Section 6 specifications of ECE Regulation No. 9 Uniform Provisions Concerning the Approval of Vehicles With Regard to Noise (October, 1968); or
  (b) the noise emitted by it is
    (i) in the case of a heavy duty vehicle, not in excess of 88 dB(A) when measured in accordance with SAE Recommended Practice J366 Exterior Sound Level For Heavy Trucks and Buses (July, 1969), and
    (ii) in the case of a light duty vehicle and an off-road utility vehicle, not in excess of 86 dB(A) when measured in accordance with SAE Standard J986a Sound Level for Passenger Cars and Light Trucks (July, 1968).

Note that these maximum permissible levels are 2 dB(A) higher than the limits set by California for vehicles manufactured after January 1, 1973, and in fact, correspond closely with maximum allowable levels established by Section 23130 of the California Vehicle Code for vehicles already on the road. Obviously, the Canadian regulations will not be successful in achieving a significant reduction in motor vehicle noise in the years ahead.

Effective noise control requires, of course, not only the necessary legislation but proper enforcement, which in turn requires the necessary equipment and trained personnel. Sound level meters are readily available today and relatively easy to use. The California Highway Patrol has trained and equipped six teams of its officers with sound level meters. The "state of the art" is now approaching that of radar speed measurements, which are accepted by the courts. As with all technical measurements, certain precautions are necessary of course. Since a sound level meter records the total sound level at any given time, the background level should be established before measurements are made on a particular source, and the total sound level should be at least 10 dB above background. If the total noise level is less than 10 dB but greater than 3 dB above background and the background level is constant during the measurement, a correction can be applied to the measurement for the background contribution. If the wind velocity at the microphone exceeds 5 mph a windscreen should be used, and measurements should not be attempted if the wind velocity exceeds 25 mph. Attention must also be paid to the presence of nearby reflecting surfaces such as buildings. While the presence of reflecting surfaces near the microphone would increase the measured sound level, a human observer at the same location would also experience a somewhat higher noise level. Perhaps, therefore, city sidewalks should be legitimate measuring locations and the burden of compliance should be placed on the vehicle operator who may have to operate his vehicle in a somewhat more careful manner. In the noise statutes discussed earlier, the specified distance between the vehicle and the microphone varied between 15 and 50 feet. From a technical viewpoint the longer distance is preferable since the vehicle then behaves more nearly like a point source. However, this advantage can be offset by practical problems such as finding measurement locations on public right-of-way. Nevertheless, if some care is exercised, the early enforcement difficulties experienced by the Metropolitan Toronto government should no longer be a problem.

Part of the opposition to effective control of noise generated by motorcycles, sports cars, and snowmobiles stems from the fact that some immature people unfortunately equate noise production with power and delight in both. Yet, sound energy constitutes an exceedingly small fraction of the energy produced by an engine. A noisy motorcycle that produces a 100 dB(A) noise level 60 feet away converts less than 0.04 hp to acoustical power. Nevertheless, the manufacturers, in appealing to some of mankind's basest emotions, continue to advertise noise, speed, and power. Of one of its 1970 models, Triumph says, "This is the fire-eater that puts the 'scram' in scrambler." Harley-Davidson advertises its mufflers as "Another 1970 change that adds a new appearance as well as added performance." Honda, in 1970, introduced a new 4-cylinder monstrosity that has four exhaust pipes and four separate mufflers—hardly an exhaust system designed to minimize noise. In merchandizing this machine, Honda proclaims, "Performance is the most terrific ever. The 68 hp overhead camshaft engine delivers power—for speeds of more than 125 mph." If the average American car, weighing about 4,000 pounds were to equal the power-to-weight ratio of this motorcycle, it would need a 550 hp engine. Despite the obvious fact that such machines are grossly overpowered, some motorcycle manufacturers claim that more effective mufflers would reduce engine power. Just as the automakers have been able to reduce air pollutants when forced to do so, motorcycle manufacturers could build much quieter machines. While there appears to be little purchaser power for quiet motorcycles, there is no technical reason why a motorcycle should produce a sound level in excess of 70 dB(A) at 50 feet. Unfortunately, the attitudes and advertising campaigns of the manufacturers indicate that such reductions will not be made voluntarily.

In Canada and the northern states of the United States, snowmobiles constitute a similar problem. Their 2-cycle engines sound like a runaway chain saw, and in the stillness of a winter wilderness, the noise can be heard for miles. An additional complication in the regulation of snowmobiles lies in the fact that they are usually operated off public roads, but that, in many respects, only aggravates the noise nuisance. There would seem to be three approaches to the snowmobile problem:

1. Federal, state, or provincial governments should immediately set maximum allowable noise limits for new snowmobiles offered for sale. (There is no justification for this limit to exceed 60 dB(A).)

In the United States, the Noise Control Act of 1972 may lead to the establishment of federal noise regulations for new snowmobiles, although the promulgation of such standards would be at the discretion of EPA.

Section 1204 of the Canada Motor Vehicle Safety Regulations, which became effective February 1, 1972, establishes an 82 dB(A) noise limit for new snowmobiles sold in Canada when the noise is measured in accordance with SAE Recommended Practice J192 Exterior Sound Level for Snowmobiles. Unfortunately, this 82 dB(A) limit corresponds more closely to present snowmobile noise levels than to a desirable and reasonably attainable goal.[17]

2. Maximum allowable noise limits should be established for snowmobiles operated on public roads. Separate criteria should be established for new and existing machines.
3. Operation of snowmobiles on public lands needs desperately to be restricted to certain well-defined locations, perhaps designated areas near winter sports centers, so that skiers, wilderness users, and rural residents are not assaulted by this unnecessary noise.

While it is true that the snowmobile now constitutes a basic mode of winter transportation for some native populations in Alaska and northern Canada, only an extremely small percentage of snowmobiles are used for that purpose. The rest are used almost exclusively for recreational activities, rather than to satisfy a basic transportation need.

Finally, governmental bodies at all levels should be giving much more serious consideration to transportation needs and energy requirements beyond the turn of the century than is presently the case, because a reasonable anticipation of such requirements should influence our policy decisions during the next ten to twenty years. In both the United States and Canada, transportation of people is largely confined to the private automobile and the airplane, both of which are noisy and neither of which is very efficient from an energy utilization standpoint. In 1970 the U.S. Congress set stringent new emission requirements for automobiles sold in the United States after January 1975—requirements which the internal combustion engine may not be able to meet and which may therefore lead to new power plants for private vehicles. Substitution of an alternate power source such as the fuel cell, the steam engine, or electrical power for the internal combustion engine would not only reduce our air pollution problems, but would yield much quieter vehicles, since the engine is in one way or another responsible for most of the noise from a motor vehicle.

In our effort to accommodate the private automobile we have built bigger and better highways, but the noise and congestion only worsen. If urban population densities continue to increase, the sheer congestion of vehicular traffic will ultimately overwhelm us. Indeed, some cities now ban vehicular traffic on certain downtown streets. Quiet, underground mass transit systems coupled with small vehicles powered by battery or fuel cell would enormously reduce traffic noise. As evidenced by the Toronto and Montreal systems, mass transit does not have to generate the screeches, squeals, and rumbles that characterize the New York and Boston subway systems.

6 Aircraft Noise

Since the introduction of commercial jet transports in 1958, the aircraft noise problem, though most acute around major airports, has become very widespread. In both the United States and Canada, aircraft noise has invaded parks and wilderness areas. In the back country of Yosemite National Park in California only an occasional air transport could be heard ten years ago. Today, Yosemite lies directly beneath one of the major jet routes between San Francisco and the East Coast. Millions of people in all economic classes are affected by this aural assault and, unfortunately, unless immediate positive action is taken by governmental bodies, there is no relief in sight. In fact, all present indications suggest a further deterioration of the situation.

For the rating of aircraft noise, a different scale, Perceived Noise Level (PNL), which takes into account the subjective response of individuals to "noisiness," was developed by K.D. Kryter of the Stanford Research Institute. Perceived Noise Level (PNL), which provides a single rating number for aircraft noise, is calculated from an octave or 1/3-octave band analysis of the noise spectrum at the instant of maximum intensity during the flyover, and the results are expressed in perceived noise decibels (PNdB).[a] An approximate PNL can be obtained with a sound level meter equipped with a special "N" weighting network. Also, for noise produced by existing fixed-wing aircraft, an approximate perceived noise level, expressed in PNdB, can be obtained by adding 13 dB to the measured dB(A) value obtained with a sound level meter equipped with the usual A-weighting network. Thus, 112 PNdB is equivalent to approximately 99 dB(A). At present, PNL is used almost exclusively for rating aircraft noise. Correlations between subjective responses and PNdB do not appear significantly better for other noises than similar correlations with A-weighting or other scales. To provide a standard rating scale for use by regulatory bodies, manufacturers, and the airline industry, the International Standards Organization (ISO) adopted PNL as the international standard for aircraft noise.

Quite recently, still another scale, Effective Perceived Noise Level (EPNL), has been employed by the U.S. Federal Aviation Administration and by the International Civil Aviation Organization (ICAO) with headquarters in Montreal. The new aircraft noise certification standards adopted by the FAA and the International Standards and Recommended Practices on Aircraft Noise adopted

---

[a]Details of this calculation, which are somewhat beyond the scope of the present work, can be found in the HANDBOOK OF NOISE MEASUREMENT listed in the reference material for this chapter.[1]

as Annex 16 to the Convention on International Civil Aviation by ICAO in 1971 are expressed in terms of this scale. EPNL consists essentially of PNL corrected for the presence of discrete frequencies (pure tones) and the duration of the flyover, and the units are expressed in effective perceived noise decibels (EPNdB).[b] For existing turbojet and turbofan civil aircraft, values of PNL usually exceed those of EPNL by 0-5 dB.

Noise levels in some communities near major airports have become so intolerable that many residents cannot continue to live in those communities. This situation illustrates what is perhaps the basic conflict over aircraft noise, namely that one group of people enjoys the economic benefits of the air transportation industry while a different group, which derives no such benefits is subjected to the noise. As a result of the obvious unfairness of this situation, by 1970 law suits totalling several hundred million dollars had been filed in U.S. courts. A few people have been awarded damages where it was shown that property values had declined or where some directly measurable economic penalty had been incurred. But generally, the private citizen has been able to get little compensation for the abuse he has suffered. Part of the difficulty arises from the fact that local communities afflicted by aircraft noise usually have no legal power to regulate the source.

U.S. courts have held that the federal government has preempted the field of air traffic regulation. A 1963 ordinance of Hempstead, Long Island, which prohibited the operation of aircraft over the city in a manner that would produce a noise level in excess of certain limits on the ground was ruled invalid in a 1966 court suit on the grounds that legislative regulation of aircraft procedures based on the exercise of local police power is a field which has been preempted by the federal government. The decision was upheld by the U.S. Court of Appeals for the Second Circuit in 1968 and the U.S. Supreme Court declined to hear the case.[5,6] Ordinances such as the one adopted by the city of Santa Barbara, California, in 1967 banning supersonic flights over the city would also probably be declared invalid in a court test.

Aircraft noise suits filed in U.S. courts have traditionally been based on such legal theories as nuisance, trespass, taking, and constitutional damaging. Suits based upon the nuisance theory have had little success, principally because the nuisance theory involves the weighing of the disturbance caused by operation of the airport against the public benefits of air transportation, and the courts have recognized the existence of a "legalized nuisance." The notion of legalized nuisance was succinctly stated by Lyman M. Tondel, Jr., as follows:

Where a public or quasi-public enterprise, like a railroad, or a power plant, or gas works, or a service system, or any irrigation system or thruway or an airport, or

[b]The actual mathematical calculation of EPNL is quite complicated, and the interested reader should consult the FAA report, AIRCRAFT NOISE EVALUATION or U.S. FAA Regulations, Part 36, or the ICAO's Annex 16, AIRCRAFT NOISE, all of which are listed in the reference material at the end of this chapter.[2,3,4]

the like is expressly authorized by legislation, nuisance claims that arise out of its proper operation are to be denied. The theory is that even if the activity in question would, if privately conducted, constitute a nuisance, it has been legalized by the legislative body which, within constitutional limits, authorized the particular conduct on behalf of the public.[7]

The trespass theory has also proven unsuccessful. In the first place, the property owner would have to prove actual invasion of his property (the airspace above his land) by the intruding aircraft. Secondly, the operator of the intruding aircraft would have to be named as defendant, and his identify could be difficult to ascertain.

According to early common law, ownership of property extended up to the sky (*ad coelum* concept). Such a concept was clearly incompatible with commercial aviation, and the U.S. Congress, in passing the Air Commerce Act in 1926, declared:

Air space above the minimum safe altitudes of flight prescribed by the Secretary of Commerce under Section 3, and such navigable air space shall be subject to a public right of freedom of interstate and foreign air navigation, in conformity with the requirement of the Act.[8]

The Secretary of Commerce, in implementing this Act, required aircraft to maintain 1,000 feet altitude above populated areas and 500 feet elsewhere and thus effectively put an end to *ad coelum* ownership. In the now famous 1946 *United States* v. *Causby* decision, the U.S. Supreme Court settled the matter, saying that ownership to the sky had no place in the modern world.[9]

In passing the Federal Aviation Act in 1958, Congress declared:

There is hereby recognized and declared to exist in behalf of any citizen of the United States a public right of freedom of transit through the navigable airspace of the United States.

The Act defines navigable airspace as that ". . . above minimum altitudes of flight prescribed by regulations issued under this chapter, and shall include airspace needed to insure safety in take-off and landing of aircraft."

Nevertheless, the courts have recognized the right of landowners to just compensation for the taking of private property for public use. In the *Causby* decision the court held that military flights directly over the owner's land were so frequent and at such low altitudes as to effectively destroy the beneficial use of the farm and that the owner was entitled to compensation.[7,10]

In the *Causby* case, the U.S. government owned both the aircraft and the airport involved. In subsequent cases involving civilian aircraft some question arose as to which party was legally liable: the airport operator, the airline that operated the offending aircraft, or the federal government which sanctioned the operation and regulated the flight pattern. In 1962, in *Griggs* v. *Allegheny Airport*, the U.S. Supreme Court held that the airport operator was liable for the "taking" of private property as a result of aircraft overflying it. In rendering its decision, the Court held that it is the airport operator who causes the disturbance in the first place. Local authorities and not the federal government decide whether an airport is to be built, and if so, where it is to be located. It is highly significant that in both this case and the *Causby* case, the flights were directly overhead, and in both instances the owners found it necessary to move from their homes because they were no longer suitable for residential use.[10,11]

In 1962, in *Batten* v. *United States,* the plaintiffs claimed significant impairment of the use and enjoyment of their property as a result of aircraft activity at a nearby Air Force base, although the homes were not directly beneath the flight path. A lower court denied the petition and the Tenth Circuit Court sustained the lower court decision.[12]

More recently some state courts have extended the interpretation to lateral as well as direct overhead flights, reasoning that lateral noise constitutes as much of an infringement on the use and enjoyment of an owner's property as does overhead noise. Other state courts, however, have followed the *Batten* precedent, and at the moment, the matter has not been resolved.[13]

If there is one lesson to be learned from the U.S. experience with aircraft noise, it is that legal remedies have been largely ineffective. The major reason why U.S. courts have been reluctant to use the taking theory as a basis for awarding compensatory damages appears to be that possible extensions of the doctrine seem limitless. If aircraft noise constitutes a basis for recovery, noise from freeways and construction (particularly public works projects) should also. In the past, at least, litigation has been initiated only after a particular facility was in operation or a particular technology was employed, and the courts have been reluctant to order such a facility closed or the use of a particular technology discontinued after the expenditure of vast sums of money, often by public agencies. Aircraft noise has become a worldwide problem that involves commercial and private aircraft traversing international boundaries, and it can never be resolved through litigation of each individual controversy.

In order to gain some insight into the nature and scope of the aircraft noise problem, let us consider the sources of aircraft noise and noise levels associated with take-off and landing profiles. The principal noise source in the turbojet engine is the jet exhaust stream (see Figure 6-1). Jet exhaust noise results from the turbulence produced by the mixing of the high velocity jet exhaust with the surrounding air. This noise extends over a wide range of the audible spectrum with most of the sound energy concentrated in the region of 100 to 1,000 Hz. Since the noise level varies with the relative velocity of the jet exhaust, one finds that an almost linear relation exists between noise level and engine thrust for this type of engine. In Figure 6-2, the composite noise level and the exhaust jet and compressor components are shown as a function of engine thrust. A number of noise suppressors designed to reduce the shear gradient between the jet exhaust stream and the surrounding air, increase the mixing zone, etc., have been

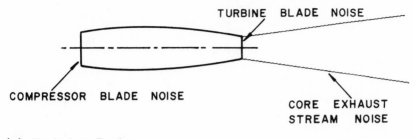

(a) Turbojet Engine

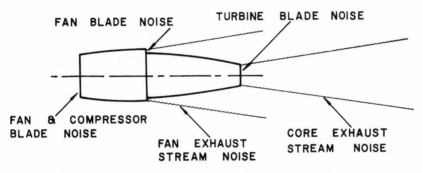

(b) Turbofan Engine

Figure 6-1. Principal Sources of Noise from Turbojet and Turbofan Aircraft Engines.

developed but have achieved only limited success. Since most of this noise is actually generated behind the aircraft, it cannot be substantially alleviated by acoustical absorbing materials in the engine itself. Only through a reduction in the velocity of the jet exhaust can this noise be substantially reduced, and for this reason the turbofan engine was developed. In the turbofan engine, the primary jet drives the compressor, as it does in the turbojet, and also a fan. A large proportion of the propulsive air drawn through the fan actually bypasses the compressor and combustion chamber (see Figure 6-1). The thrust is supplied by both the primary jet and the fan exhaust stream, and the mixing of these two streams provides a lower velocity exhaust and consequently less noise. Unfortunately, however, the presence of the fan introduces a new noise source in the turbofan engine. In Figure 6-3 the composite noise level and the levels associated

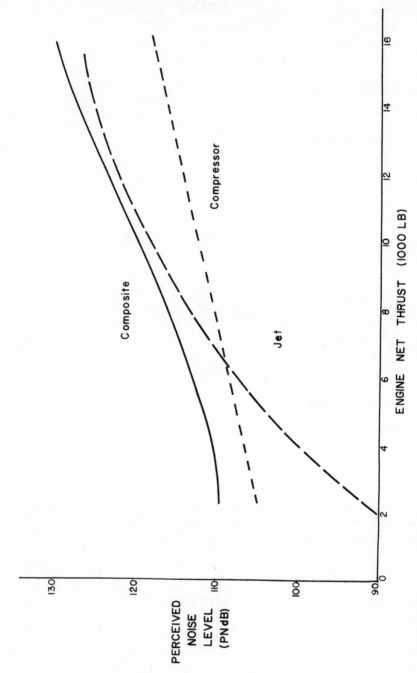

Figure 6-2. Composite Noise Level and the Levels Produced by the Exhaust Jet and Compressor of a Turbojet Engine at 400-Foot Altitude.[16]

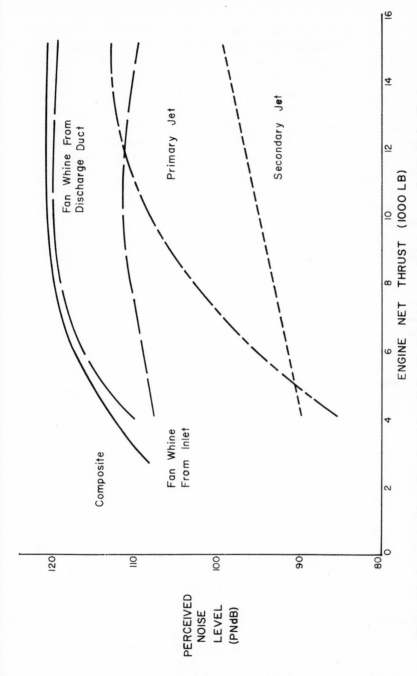

Figure 6-3. Composite Noise Level and Levels Produced by Various Components of a Turbofan Engine at 400-Foot Altitude.[16]

with the various components are shown as a function of engine thrust. The overall noise level produced by this engine does not increase markedly with engine thrust, and at high thrust values, it is lower than that of the turbojet. However, at lower engine thrust, the overall noise level produced by the turbofan engine is somewhat higher than that of the turbojet, and furthermore, the predominate noise source in the turbofan is no longer the broad band jet exhaust noise, but some higher frequency "pure tone" components produced by the passage of air through the inlet guide vanes, the fan, compressor, and ducts. This noise is frequently called "fan whine" and is related to the number of blades and frequencies of rotation of the fan and compressor. Since the noise is generated in the engine itself, it is amenable to attenuation by engine design and acoustical absorbers.[14,15,16]

Since engine thrust is much higher on take-off than on landing, the above considerations help explain why landing noise is different in character from take-off noise and is frequently more annoying. Figure 6-4 shows a typical take-off flight profile and corresponding noise levels on the ground directly

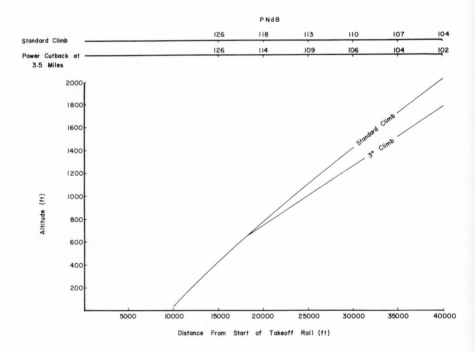

Figure 6-4. Typical Take-Off Flight Profile for a Four-Engine Turbojet Aircraft in Standard and 3-Degree Climb Attitude on a Standard Day. Note: Perceived noise levels on the ground directly beneath the flight path are shown along the top edge of the graph. On a hot day the noise level will be as much as 4 PNdB higher because of reduced rate of climb.

under the flight path of a large four-engine turbojet aircraft on a standard day. On a hot day, the noise levels may be as much as 4 PNdB higher because of reduced rate of climb. The corresponding values for turbofan aircraft will be about 5 PNdB lower than the values shown on the graph.

That one does not have to be directly under the flight path of a large jet on take-off in order to receive an ear-splitting roar is shown by Figure 6-5 where noise level contours for a four-engine turbojet on take-off have been plotted. From Figure 6-4 we see that when such a plane is six miles from the point of brake release at the end of the runway, it has attained an altitude of about 1,520 feet, and from Figure 6-5 we see that the noise level on the ground one mile on either side of the flight path is nearly 95 PNdB.

A similar situation exists on landing, with two important exceptions. On take-off, engine thrust is high and the angle of climb usually exceeds 4 degrees. Since engine thrust is lower on landing, the overall noise level is considerably lower for turbojet aircraft, but the predominate noise is now the compressor whine. In the case of fanjet aircraft, the overall noise level is only slightly lower, and fan whine constitutes the major component of this noise. Furthermore, during final approach into most airports, jet aircraft descend in a 3-degree glide slope, as shown in Figure 6-6, where altitude has been plotted as a function of distance from threshold (the end of the runway closest to the approaching aircraft). Consequently, whereas the departing jet had attained an altitude of 1,520 feet when it was 6 miles from the point of brake release at the end of the runway, an approaching aircraft would fly over this same point in the community at an altitude of less than 1,200 feet. In the case of turbofan aircraft, the noise level on the ground directly beneath the flight path at this point would be about 104 PNdB for both take-off and landing. On balance, then, landing noise is frequently as much of a problem as take-off noise, and we can readily see that if either take-offs or approaches are made over a populated area, a large number of people will be subjected to high noise levels.[17]

The situation at Los Angeles International Airport is instructive in this regard. Los Angeles International Airport (LAX) is owned and operated by the City of Los Angeles. During fiscal year 1968-1969 there were more than 630,000 take-offs and landings, an average of over 1,700 per day, and the airport handled almost 21 million people. Figure 6-7 shows the usual traffic pattern at LAX superimposed on a map of the area. Except during periods of adverse winds, take-offs are made over water to the west. A portion of the community of Playa del Rey is situated atop the bluffs overlooking the water between the end of the runway and the ocean. Noise levels in this community frequently exceed 120 PNdB. There is, however, a much larger aspect of the problem. All but a small percentage of the aircraft departing LAX are destined for points north or east of Los Angeles and hence must recross the coastline. Except during the nighttime hours 9 A.M. to 7 A.M., nearly all of these aircraft recross the coastline along a 30 mile stretch between Malibu and the Palos Verdes Peninsula. Because of

92

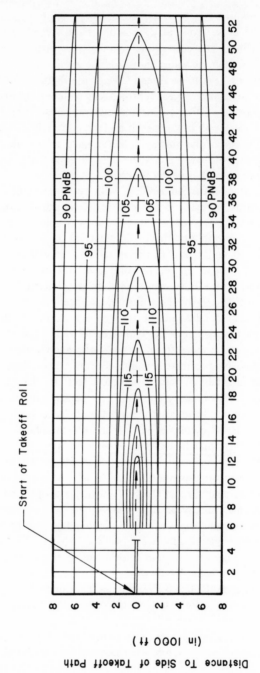

Distance From Start of Takeoff Roll (in 1000 ft)

Note: For Civil Turbojet Aircraft use contours as shown.
For Civil Turbofan Aircraft reduce contour values by 5 PNdB.

Figure 6-5. Noise Level Contours on the Ground for a Four-Engine Turbojet Aircraft on Take-Off on a Standard Day.[18]

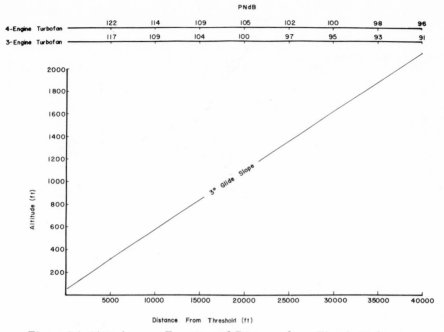

Figure 6-6. Altitude as a Function of Distance from Threshold for a Standard 3-Degree Glide Slope Approach. Note: Perceived noise levels on the ground directly beneath the flight path for 4-engine turbofan and 3-engine turbofan aircraft are shown along the top edge of the graph.

variations in aircraft type, take-off weight, and flight path, the altitude at which the aircraft recross the coastline varies between about 4,000 and 15,000 feet. Resulting noise levels in commumities along the coast sometimes exceed 90 PNdB. Many of these communities are quiet residential neighborhoods where the daytime ambient noise level is 50-60 PNdB. In such communities, aircraft flyover noise, although by no means as intense as in Playa del Rey, nevertheless constitutes a serious invasion.[19]

From Figure 6-7 we can also gain some appreciation of the noise problems created by landing aircraft. The approaches are made over a populated area, nearly all of it residential in character. When an approaching turbofan aircraft crosses Harbor Freeway, it is approximately 6 miles from touchdown, its altitude is about 1,700 feet, and from Figure 6-6 we find that the noise level on the ground beneath the flight path is nearly 100 PNdB—the approximate equivalent of a diesel truck passing by 50 feet away. In a school playground near the San Diego Freeway, the noise level often exceeds 120 PNdB. Clearly, therefore, noise from aircraft operations at LAX is by no means confined to a

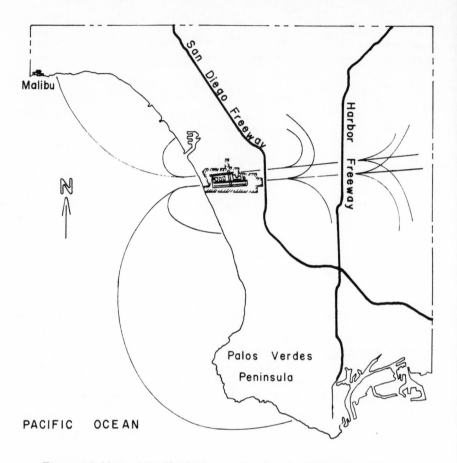

Figure 6-7. Normal Traffic Pattern at Los Angeles International Airport Superimposed on a Map of the Area. Note: Normally, approaches are made from the east, and take-offs are made over water to the west.

well-defined area in close proximity to the airport, but actually intrudes into a large percentage of the Los Angeles basin.

Various spokesmen for the air transportation industry and the Federal Aviation Administration have suggested that people adapt to aircraft noise. However, a number of aircraft noise studies have clearly shown that people become more intolerant of jet aircraft as the number of flyovers is increased. The results of one such investigation indicate that if the level of tolerance is judged by a noise environment which will produce vigorous individual complaints and possible concerted group action, then people will tolerate a peak noise level of about 115 PNdB if only one flyover occurs per day. However, this tolerance level falls to 100 PNdB if there are 32 flyovers per day and to 94 PNdB if the number of flyovers increases to 128 per day.[20,21,22]

These findings are substantiated by the results of our own survey of residents near LAX.

One resident explained, "We don't really adapt. However, I can sleep through the jets, but my parents cannot. We have put earphones on our television and stereo, but it is impossible to adapt effectively to the noise." An art professor at California State College, Los Angeles said, "Stay indoors, sleep with ear plugs, try to make a joke of it, become more and more neurotic."

Some authorities have suggested soundproofing of homes as a way to make living near airports more acceptable. Most residents in the survey rejected soundproofing as a solution, saying they did not reside in California just to live in a soundproof box.

A very large percentage of the residents near the airport want to relocate but are unable to do so. In the first place very few prospective home buyers would even consider purchasing these homes and the situation is further complicated by the reluctance of lending institutions to loan money on such property. Furthermore, the homeowners cannot qualify for second mortgage loans when assets are tied up in unsalable property.

In a precedent-setting opinion, a Los Angeles Superior Court in February of 1970 awarded more than $740,000 to 539 property owners near LAX. The court held that the owners were entitled to payment by the city for the loss of full enjoyment of their property. Since most airports are owned by governmental bodies, the increasing number of suits arising from aircraft noise will put additional economic and political pressures on local governments to alleviate the problem.

Short of closing the airport, the operator of an established airport can take only a limited number of steps to reduce the noise level in surrounding communities. When commercial jets first came into service in 1958, the New York Port Authority ruled that aircraft using Kennedy International Airport must be operated in such a manner that the noise level in communities under the flight path on take-off does not exceed 112 PNdB. In no U.S. cities other than New York are noise limits on take-offs known to be in effect at the present time. Many nations in western Europe including Norway (at Oslo's Fornebu airport only), Sweden, Switzerland, and West Germany have also adopted the 112 PNdB limit for take-off noise. At London's Heathrow Airport, departing aircraft are now limited to 110 PNdB during daytime hours and 102 PNdB at night in the first major residential area overflown after take-off.

While many residents of communities situated near New York's Kennedy Airport consider the 112 PNdB barrage intolerable, the fact is that appreciably lower noise levels cannot be attained in those communities with existing aircraft. Furthermore, at most major airports residential developments are situated so near the runways that existing aircraft could probably not comply with a 112 PNdB noise limitation on overflights of such communities. Aircraft departing Seattle-Tacoma International Airport, for example, overfly a residential area only 17,000 feet from the start of take-off roll, and similar situations exist elsewhere. Very recently, however, the Airport Operators' Council International, to which most major airport operators belong, has set noise limits for new aircraft entering service which are equal at least to those specified in the new U.S. Federal Aviation Regulations, Part 36, which will be discussed shortly. The only aircraft now in service to which these limits apply are the McDonnell-Douglas DC-10, the Lockheed L-1011 and those Boeing 747 airplanes manufactured after March 1, 1972. Sidney Goldstein, general counsel for the New York Port Authority, has observed:

The only way to solve the noise problem is at the source, the jet engine. This solution requires federal money as well as the close cooperation of the Federal Aviation Administration with airframe and engine manufacturers, airlines, pilots, and airport operators. The existing situation, in which those disturbed by the roar of jets are theoretically made whole by the payment of damages, does not alleviate aircraft noise.[23]

Clearly, the airport operators regard the reduction of aircraft noise to be primarily the responsibility of the government, the airlines, and the aircraft manufacturers. The attitude of the airlines is well illustrated by some remarks made by John E. Stephen, general counsel of the Air Transport Association, at a U.S. House Commerce Committee hearing in March, 1967. He said:

If anything has been learned from the exhaustive studies made of noise complaints, it is that no matter how much the noise level is reduced there will remain an ineradicable hard-core group of complainants. Both British and American studies indicate that this constant hard-core group of complainants constitute about 30% of the population near airports. In this sense, the aircraft noise problem will probably never be solved.[24]

In the first place, of course, there have been no real reductions in aircraft noise. The reductions which have been achieved in some communities as a result of operating procedure changes have been more than offset by the increased volume of traffic. Secondly, 30 percent of the population hardly seems like an insignificant group of "nuts" whose grievances should be dismissed.

At an international conference on noise in 1966, a Boeing Company representative stated:

Until a fuller understanding of the problem is attained, the aircraft manufacturer can only continue to produce competitive designs that yield the lowest noise levels consistent with good performance of the aircraft.[16]

Boeing, at the time, was proceeding with the design of a plane incredibly worse than anything in commercial use—a supersonic transport.

Faced with a mounting crisis, what can governments do? In most nations, regulation of civil aircraft operations is vested in an agency of the national government. In the United States, regulation of civil aircraft operations is the responsibility of the FAA, and the Federal Aviation Act of 1958 empowered the

FAA to prescribe air traffic regulations for the "protection of persons and property on the ground," including air traffic regulations for noise abatement. Under this authority, the FAA has initiated air traffic control procedures at some airports designed to reduce the noise level in some nearby communities. These noise abatement procedures include the use of preferential runway systems to avoid overflying densely populated areas and power cutbacks after take-off to reduce engine thrust (see Figure 6-4).[25,26]

One example of a preferential runway system is the one now in use at San Francisco International Airport. This airport is located on the western side of San Francisco Bay and is bounded on the south and east by water. When wind conditions permit, take-offs are made on runways 1 L and 1 R, and landings are made on runways 28 L and 28 R (see Figure 6-8). Afternoon westerly winds frequently necessitate take-offs on runways 28 L and 28 R in which case the aircraft overfly residential areas shortly after take-off. For calendar year 1969, the SFO tower reports the following approximate runway usages for take-offs:

Runways 1	65%
Runways 28	25%
Runways 10	9%
Runways 19	1%

Average daily jet departures total approximately 400.

Of course, only some airports are situated in such a manner that use of a preferential runway system can diminish flights over populated areas. Other flight control procedures for noise abatement have resulted in reduced noise levels in some communities, but such reductions have seldom been substantial, and there is usually a price to be paid in terms of higher noise levels somewhere else. In May 1970, Los Angeles International Airport implemented a new nighttime departure procedure for use between the hours 9 P.M.-7 A.M. In the new procedure, aircraft destined for an easterly or southerly city take-off over water to the west in the usual manner. However, instead of making either a right-hand or left-hand turn and recrossing the coastline within a 15-mile radius of the airport, such departing aircraft make a left turn after take-off and continue south around the Palos Verdes Peninsula, recrossing the coastline at an altitude of about 18,000 feet between Long Beach and Seal Beach. This procedure was clearly welcomed by communities situated north and immediately south of the airport. However, on the Palos Verdes Peninsula, an expensive residential area, the aircraft passing just offshore produce a 60-75 PNdB noise level where the ambient nighttime noise level is less than 45 PNdB.[19]

At some airports the FAA has implemented a two-segment climb-out procedure (see Figure 6-4) in which the departing aircraft climb as rapidly as possible, using take-off power, until they reach a noise sensitive area. The power is then cut back and a lower rate of climb maintained until the aircraft is out of

98

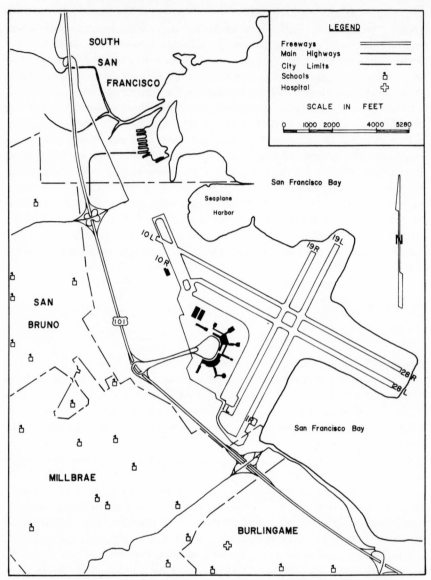

Figure 6-8. Map of San Francisco Airport and Vicinity. Note: When wind conditions permit, take-offs are made from runways 1L and 1R.

the noise sensitive area. In feasibility studies at JFK Airport the FAA found that noise levels in the sensitive communities averaged about 5 PNdB lower when this procedure was used than when the normal rate of climb was maintained. This study also showed, however, that slight changes in the power setting after the cutback had been made can increase the noise level on the ground 10 to 15

PNdB. One additional difficulty with this procedure is that more distant communities often receive higher noise exposures because the aircraft overfly such communities at lower altitudes than would be the case had the original rate of climb been maintained.[26]

Some reduction in approach noise levels could be realized from steeper glide slopes. The higher rate of descent associated with steep-gradient approach procedures results in the aircraft overflying more distant communities at a higher altitude and in a lower power setting during the approach. As a result of the higher altitude, however, the duration of the flyover is increased. Furthermore, the Air Line Pilots Association is presently opposed to procedures that require a glide slope above 3 degrees.

From the foregoing considerations we see that lower noise levels, particularly in the immediate environs of an airport, can sometimes be achieved by modification of flight procedures. Such reductions, while important, are usually not of substantial magnitude and are rapidly offset by the increasing volume of traffic. Indeed, in *Alleviation of Jet Aircraft Noise Near Airports*, a report of the Jet Aircraft Noise Panel published in 1966 by the U.S. Office of Science and Technology, Dr. Oscar Bakke of the FAA states:

Nor can it be presumed that operating procedures such as preferred runways, turns from heavily populated communities and high descents will do more than chip away the rough edges of the problems, as effective as such measures are. Given the expected continued climb in air traffic, in fact, airplane noise over New York as a whole will become worse, not better, in the next decade. And the same can undoubtedly be said for other cities.

One area in which governments at all levels need desperately to cooperate is that of land use planning around airports. Thus far, little progress has been made in this field. One of the difficulties has been that while aircraft flight procedures are usually regulated by an agency of the national government, land use around airports is usually under the jurisdiction of local government. Unfortunately, local governments have often permitted encroachment of residential development right up to the airport fence. If some of the high noise exposure areas had been zoned to exclude residential development, noise problems in the immediate airport environs would be less acute. Around many existing airports where this problem is already well progressed, some amelioration through land use zoning is not out of reach, difficult as though the task may seem. Communities change, and as buildings are removed to make way for new ones, account can be taken of the need for compatible land use and zoning regulations implemented to restrict such land to industrial or other compatible use. However, such steps require close cooperation between numerous governmental agencies.

A great deal more foresight is needed in planning new airports. In the case of new airports, the opportunity exists, through acquisition of sufficient land, to prevent encroachment of residential and other incompatible developments.

However, the problem of locating a new airport near a major metropolitan area today is at best difficult. No useful purpose is served by locating such an airport adjacent to an existing community, even though it may be some distance from the city. If a more remote location is chosen, either the facility itself or its operation may destroy or seriously impair the natural beauty of a wilderness or recreation area. Such was the case with the proposed Everglades jetport adjacent to Everglades National Park in Florida, and such will also be the case with the proposed Palmdale facility for Los Angeles. In this regard, the new Dulles International Airport near Washington, D.C., is, in some respects a model. The airport is located in a farming area about 30 miles from downtown Washington, and some 18,000 acres were purchased for the airport to prevent encroachment of residential dwellings. Because of its distance from the city, the airport is not heavily used. In 1969, 9.7 million passengers used Washington National while only 1.9 million used Dulles. If, however, a rapid transit system linked Dulles with downtown Washington, the airport would be sufficiently accessible that use of Washington National (which from the noise pollution standpoint is in an atrocious location) could be discontinued.[27] Ultimately, of course, the only solution to the aircraft noise problem that is invading every corner of the world lies in quieting or eliminating the source. Unfortunately, there is no basis for optimism that any substantial relief will be forthcoming within the next decade. The giant Boeing 747, despite a major increase in engine thrust, is about 7 EPNdB quieter on take-off than B-707 turbofan aircraft. Take-off noise levels for both the McDonnell-Douglas DC-10 and the Lockheed L-1011 are approximately 10 EPNdB lower than those of the B-747. However, landing noise levels for the DC-10 and L-1011 are roughly comparable to those of the B-747. Furthermore, both the DC-10 and L-1011 are shorter range aircraft with a smaller payload than the B-747, and even then, by 1974, these two types of aircraft will comprise only about 8 percent of the U.S. jet fleet and a smaller percentage of the Canadian jet fleet. Table 6-1 shows the composition of the Canadian commercial air carrier fleet since 1964. Note that while the total number of aircraft in the fleet increased 57 percent during the 8-year period 1964-1972, the number of pure jet aircraft increased seven-fold. As of July 1, 1972, Air Canada was the only Canadian carrier which had ordered wide-bodied jets. It had three Boeing 747 aircraft in service and ten Lockheed L-1011s on order.

In a belated effort to spur the development of quieter aircraft, in 1968 the U.S. Congress enacted the Aircraft Noise Abatement Act (Public Law 90-411) which required the Federal Aviation Administration to undertake the control and abatement of aircraft noise. Pursuant to this legislation, in November of 1969 the FAA issued Federal Aviation Regulations (FAR), Part 36, which specifies noise standards for all subsonic transport category aircraft and all subsonic jet aircraft regardless of size for which type certificates have been filed since December 1, 1969. These standards are applicable to the McDonnell-Doug-

Table 6-1
Canadian Commercial Air Carrier Fleet

Year[1]	Total Aircraft in Fleet	Jet	Turbo-Prop	Piston	Total	Helicopters
		Fix-Wing Aircraft				Helicopters
1964	2,043	20	79	1,726	1,825	218
1965	2,157	21	75	1,801	1,897	260
1966	2,371	29	77	1,971	2,077	294
1967	2,605	40	80	2,155	2,275	330
1968	2,763	70	94	2,255	2,419	344
1969	2,883	85	97	2,335	2,517	366
1970	2,986	98	97	2,372	2,597	389
1971	3,015	130	115	2,354	2,599	416
1972	3,209	139	124	2,462	2,725	484

Source: Service Bulletin, Aviation Statistics Center, Statistics Canada, Ottawa (August 1972).
[1]Figures are given as of July 15 of each year.

las DC-10 and the Lockheed L-1011 as well as those Boeing 747 airplanes manufactured after March 1, 1972, but otherwise do not apply to existing aircraft or to new production of existing aircraft. Neither do they apply to supersonic aircraft.

The noise certification standards set forth in FAR Part 36 are expressed in effective perceived noise decibels (EPNdB) and provide that flight tests must demonstrate the airplane does not exceed the following noise limits:

(1) For takeoff, 108 EPNdB for maximum weights of 600,000 lbs. or more, less 5 EPNdB for each halving of the 600,000 lb. maximum weight down to 93 EPNdB for maximum weights of 75,000 lbs. and under. Measurements are to be recorded at a point 3.5 nautical miles (21,280 feet) from the start of take-off roll on the extended centerline of the runway.
(2) For approach and sideline, 108 EPNdB for maximum weights of 600,000 lbs. or more, less 2 EPNdB per halving of the 600,000 lb. maximum weight down to 102 EPNdB for maximum weights of 75,000 lbs. and under. Approach noise is to be recorded 1.0 nautical mile (6,080 feet) from threshold on the extended ceterline of the runway. Sideline noise is to be measured at a point 0.25 nautical miles distant from the runway centerline for aircraft powered by 3 engines or less and 0.35 nautical miles for aircraft powered by more than 3 engines.[28]

FAR Part 36 limits for take-off and landing noise along with the noise levels for several types of existing aircraft are illustrated in Figures 6-9 and 6-10. As the figures show, the FAR Part 36 noise limits vary with aircraft weight, and for

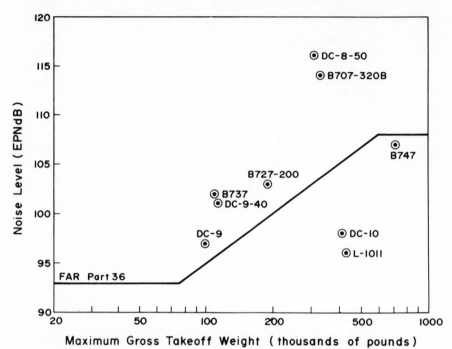

Figure 6-9. FAR Part 36 Limits for Take-Off Noise and Noise Levels for Several Types of Existing Aircraft at the FAA Measuring Point for Take-Off Noise.

airçraft having a maximum gross take-off weight of 600,000 lbs. or more, the limits are only marginally lower than the noise levels generated by today's noisiest turbofan aircraft. Since PNL is approximately 2-3 dB higher than EPNL, the 108 EPNdB limit corresponds to a PNL of about 110 PNdB, which represents an improvement over the existing New York Port Authority limits of only 2 PNdB. Reductions of this magnitude obviously offer not the slightest hope of relief for communities plagued by an already growing number of flyovers.

The figures show, too, that the noise level of the DC-10, which has a maximum gross takeoff weight of 410,000 lbs., could be 7 EPNdB higher and the aircraft would still meet FAR Part 36 requirements. We can therefore conclude with reasonable certainty that instead of providing an impetus to noise abatement technology, the FAR limits are well within the capability of existing technology. Despite the fact the aircraft industry played a major role in formulating these regulations, the Boeing Company has already begun to criticize them, claiming that its planned "stretched" version of the 747 which would hold up to 1,000 passengers, will not be able to meet the 108 EPNdB limit.[29]

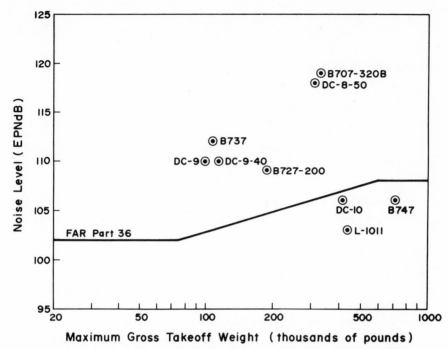

Figure 6-10. FAR Part 36 Limits for Approach Noise and Noise Levels for Several Types of Existing Aircraft at the FAA Measuring Point for Approach Noise.

There is presently no clear profit incentive for aircraft manufacturers and airlines to reduce noise nor is there any economic penalty attached to their failure to do so. The aircraft noise problem parallels the automobile pollution situation. Just as few people apparently choose a new car on the basis of air pollution control features of a particular model, it seems improbable that anyone flies from city A to city B on a particular airline solely because of the quieter engines used on that carrier's planes. The proper role of government in this situation is perhaps best enunciated by J. Donald Reilly, executive vice-president of the Airport Operators Council International, in testimony to the Subcommittee on Air and Water Pollution of the U.S. Senate on April 13, 1972:

The Government's role is of necessity an aggressive one of pushing a continuing reduction of noise levels on a continuing time scale. The Government therefore finds itself in the position of sponsoring technological progress in an area where technological progress has not occurred voluntarily.

Such an approach was recently used by Congress to force a reduction in the future levels of auto pollution. Recognizing that industry had no financial incentive to reduce pollution, Congress required that, by a given date, new automobiles be prohibited from exceeding certain pollution limits.[30]

Governments should begin immediately to set noise standards for certification of new aircraft that will force aircraft manufacturers to build much quieter airplanes. A recent Joint Report of the Department of Transportation and the National Aeronautics and Space Administration on *Civil Aviation Research and Development* (CARD Study) concluded:

It is a key recommendation of the present study that until (aircraft noise is suppressed) time-phased research goals be established calling for reduction of about 10-15 dB per decade.

This approach must provide for research goals based not on what is technically feasible but what is needed to satisfy community environmental goals.

In the testimony before the U.S. Senate Subcommittee referred to previously, Mr. J. Donald Reilly, of the Airport Operators Council International observed:

The present 108 EPNdB limit is not permanent and will not be acceptable to communities for the indefinite future; it is but a temporary stepping stone to much lower levels.[30]

Yet the FAR Part 36 limits for certification of new aircraft in the United States are still in effect, and the FAA has not indicated when, if ever, any new standards will be promulgated. Since approximately two years normally elapse between the filing of a type certificate and the time a new aircraft enters commercial service, new aircraft entering service in 1975 can still be as noisy as the present FAR Part 36 limits permit.

In its proposed rulemaking in January, 1969, the FAA proposed a "noise floor" of 80 EPNdB as "an objective to aim for, and to achieve where economically reasonable, technologically practicable, and appropriate to the particular design" and continued:

However, this objective is important because it makes it clear to all applicants that no increment of noise above 80 EPNdB can be considered acceptable, in and of itself, where it can be eliminated practically and reasonably. This figure is proposed as a reasonable boundary between noise levels that are high enough to interfere with communications and to obstruct normal life in homes or other buildings that are not designed with specific acoustical objectives, and lower noise levels which, while not completely benign, nevertheless allow those activities to proceed. Where this goal can be reached in a given case, and can be justified as economically reasonable, technologically practical, and appropriate to the particular type design, the FAA does not intend to ignore this potential reduction.[31]

Under heavy industry pressure, however, the FAA dropped the 80 EPNdB "objective" from the regulations it subsequently promulgated stating:

The FAA has determined that the request to remove the noise "floor" of 80 EPNdB from the regulatory language is reasonable and should be granted. This noise floor, not being currently achievable, could have no immediate legal effect.[28]

Because of the long lead time involved in the design and certification of new aircraft, unless future goals are set now and a schedule established for their implementation, new aircraft entering service in the late 1970s and early 1980s will still be as noisy as those of today. Such a schedule may have to be legislated into effect rather than promulgated by a regulatory agency in order to circumvent the influence which the air transportation industry has on FAA policy.

In response to a 1966 presidential directive, the President's Office of Science and Technology, in cooperation with the Federal Aviation Administration, National Aeronautics and Space Administration (NASA), and the Department of Housing and Urban Development, initiated an "Aircraft Noise Alleviation Program." As a part of this program, NASA embarked on a project to "identify promising nacelle modifications on current four-engine turbofan powered aircraft that would reduce the noise under the approach path by 15 PNdB." NASA contractors completed the study in October 1969 and reported that retrofitting existing jet aircraft could achieve a reduction in approach noise of 10.5 to 12 EPNdB for DC-8 aircraft and a reduction of 15.5 EPNdB for the Boeing 707s. A smaller reduction in take-off noise could also be realized (a 2 to 3.5 EPNdB reduction for DC-8 aircraft and 3 EPNdB for the B-707s).[30]

In July 1970, the Rohr Corp. of Chula Vista, California, completed a study for the FAA on the economic impact of implementing a retrofit program. The Rohr studies concluded that a retrofit program could reduce approach noise by 10 EPNdB for the B-727, B-737, and DC-9 aircraft and by 13 EPNdB for the B-707 and DC-8 type aircraft. The retrofit program plus power reductions after take-off would reduce take-off noise by 8 EPNdB for the four-engine turbofan aircraft (B-707 and DC-8) and by 5 EPNdB for the two- and three-engine turbofans. Cost estimates provided in the Rohr study depend on two variables: configuration and materials used. Four different configurations, each of which provides a successively greater degree of noise reduction, were considered.[32]

Table 6-2 shows the approximate present noise levels, at the FAA measuring points, of the turbofan aircraft considered for retrofitting and the estimated noise reductions required to bring the noise levels within the FAR Part 36 limits of 108 EPNdB. (Although the retrofitted noise levels exceed 108 EPNdB in a few cases, FAR Part 36 Regulations permit small excess deviations at one measuring point to be offset by corresponding reductions at other points.) Because of the high noise levels generated by the four-engine aircraft, only configuration 4, the most drastic modification considered in the Rohr study, could provide the necessary degree of noise reduction. For the two- and three-engine aircraft, a relatively slight modification (configuration 1) would suffice. The estimated noise reductions shown in Table 6-2 are also based upon the use of material A, the least expensive and apparently least effective of the four materials considered in the Rohr study.[33]

Cost estimates from the Rohr study for retrofitting each type of aircraft are shown in Table 6-3. The more drastic modifications required on the four-engine aircraft are reflected in the higher costs shown for these planes.

Table 6-2

Noise Levels of Turbofan Aircraft in Current U.S. Air Carrier Fleet, Estimated Noise Reductions from the Rohr Study, and Noise Levels of These Aircraft After Retrofitting

Aircraft Type	Noise Levels (EPNdB)		
	Approach	Takeoff	Sideline
Four-engine (Retrofit configuration 4)			
Boeing 707	119	114	108
	−12.0	−5.5	−4.0
	107.0	108.5	104.0
Boeing 720	118	104	108
	−12.0	−5.5	−4.0
	106.0	98.5	104.0
DC-8	118	116	106
	−12.0	−6.0	−4.0
	106.0	110.0	102.0
Two- and Three-engine (Retrofit configuration 1)			
Boeing 727	109	103	105
	−1.5	−1.0	−1.0
	107.5	102.0	104.0
Boeing 737	112	102	104
	−7.0	−1.5	−1.5
	105.0	100.5	102.5
DC-9	110	97	105
	−1.5	−1.0	−1.0
	108.5	96.0	104.0
BAC-111	106	103	108
	−1.5	−1.0	−1.0
	104.5	102.0	107.0

Source: M.R. Segal, "Aircraft Noise: The Retrofitting Approach," Science Policy Research Division, Congressional Research Service, Rept. 72-78SP, HE9901 (March 1972).

In order to calculate the total cost for retrofitting the entire U.S. commerical air carrier fleet, one has to make some assumptions about the number of aircraft to be retrofitted. Table 6-4 gives the number of jet aircraft in service and on order by the 39 certificated U.S. route air carriers as of December 31, 1970. Aircraft of supplemental (charter and nonscheduled airlines), intrastate, and

Table 6-3
Cost Estimates for Retrofitting Existing Types of Turbofan Aircraft[1]

Aircraft	Cost per Aircraft[2]
Boeing 707 and 720	$924,000
DC-8-50 and DC-8-61	998,000
DC-8-62 and DC-8-63	926,000
Boeing 727	100,000
Boeing 737	137,000
DC-9 and BAC-111	74,000

[1]Cost estimates derived from: "Economic Impact of Implementing Acoustically Treated Nacelle and Duct Configurations Applicable to Low By-pass Turbofan Engines," FAA Rept. 70-11, Rohr Corp., Chula Vista, California (July, 1970).
[2]The Rohr study differentiated between various models of DC-8 aircraft because of significant differences in retrofitting costs.

foreign flag carriers are not included. The table shows that on December 31, 1970, there were 2,064 jet aircraft available for service, none of which met FAR Part 36 standards. Furthermore, 821 of these were very noisy four-engine aircraft. If a retrofitting program were implemented, not all of these aircraft would be retrofitted. In the first place, 199 of these planes are turbojets which cannot be modified in the fashion just described. The cost of replacing four engines in addition to other modifications would dictate their retirement. Secondly, it has been widely assumed by the FAA, the Air Transport Association, and others, that by 1975, some of the older, lower-capacity four-engine turbofan aircraft (such as the Boeing 720-B) will be replaced by the wide-body tri-jets (DC-10 and L-1011). The estimates of the number of older aircraft in the fleet in 1975 vary widely, however, and the rate of replacement has not been nearly as rapid as most estimates indicated. Table 6-5 gives the cost of retrofitting the existing fleet of turbofan aircraft of the U.S. certificated route air carriers in service on December 31, 1970. The total cost is $695 million, of which $585 million or 84 percent is required to retrofit 622 noisy four-engine aircraft. The cost is clearly substantial, but some perspective is afforded by the fact that in 1970, the air carriers spent $1.1 billion on sales and promotion.[34]

NASA recently started work on an advanced retrofit system which would be more costly than the system previously considered but which would provide substantial improvements in noise reduction. For the noisy four-engine turbofan aircraft, NASA predicts noise reductions of up to 17 EPNdB on approach, 15 EPNdB on take-off, and 10 EPNdB on sideline noise. For two- and three-engine turbofan aircraft, noise reductions of 12 to 14 EPNdB are anticipated. NASA estimates that this retrofit system will cost about $130 million to develop and approximately $500,000 per engine to install—significantly greater than the cost of the lower performance systems considered previously.[30,33]

The question of implementing a retrofit program for the commercial air carrier fleet is a political decision which involves many intangible factors as well

Table 6-4

Number of Jet Aircraft in Service on December 31, 1970 and Number of Additional Aircraft on Order by the 39 Certificated U.S. Route Air Carriers[1]

Aircraft Type[2]	Number Available for Service Dec. 31, 1970[3]	Number on Order Dec. 31, 1970[3]
Boeing 707	402	–
Boeing 720	115	–
DC-8	263	3
Convair-880/990	41	–
Total Four-engine Conventional	821	3
Boeing 727	629	6
Boeing 737	133	–
DC-9	324	7
BAC-111	67	–
Caravelle SE-210	15	–
Total 2 & 3-engine Conventional	1168	13
Boeing 747	75	39
Total Four-engine Wide-body	75	39
DC-10	0	86
L-1011	0	105
Total Three-engine Wide-body	0	191

[1]U.S. certificated route air carriers do not include supplemental carriers (charter airlines), intrastate, or foreign flag carriers.

[2]In some cases, the aircraft listed has a number of different models. Where this situation exists, all models have been included under the single type shown. For example, the DC-8 category includes the DC-8-10,-20,-30,-50,-61,-62,-63,-F, and -63F.

[3]HANDBOOK OF AIRLINE STATISTICS, 1971 ed., Bureau of Accounts & Statistics, U.S. Civil Aeronautics Board, Washington, D.C. (1972).

as economic ones. There is no real way to measure, in economic terms, the disruption that aircraft noise causes in the lives of the approximately 7¼ million Americans living in airport environments.[33,35]

Even though the NASA and Rohr studies of 1969 and 1970 clearly demonstrated the technological feasibility of retrofitting, the FAA has begun another comprehensive study of retrofitting which will not be completed until the end of 1973. Because of the obvious lack of enthusiasm which the FAA displays for noise reduction, the Subcommittee on Air and Water Pollution of the U.S. Senate Public Works Committee considered adding language to the Noise Control Act of 1972 which would have required that by January 1, 1976 all existing jet aircraft either be retrofitted to meet FAR Part 36 standards or retired. Although this proposal was not adopted, the responses to it elucidated

Table 6-5

Cost of Retrofitting the Existing Fleet of Turbofan Aircraft of the Certificated U.S. Route Air Carriers

Aircraft	Number in Service[1] (Dec. 31, 1970)	Cost per Aircraft	Total Cost (Millions of Dollars)
Boeing 707 & 720	430	$924,000	397
DC-8-50 & DC-8-61	137	998,000	137
DC-8-62 & DC-8-63	55	926,000	51
Boeing 727	629	100,000	63
Boeing 737	133	137,000	18
DC-9 & BAC-111	391	74,000	29
Total	1,775		695

[1] Number of turbofan aircraft of each type in service on December 31, 1970 by the certificated U.S. route air carriers obtained from HANDBOOK OF AIRLINE STATISTICS, Bureau of Accounts & Statistics, U.S. Civil Aeronautics Board, Washington, D.C. (January, 1972).

the positions of various segments of the air transportation industry on retrofitting. The Airport Operators Council International warmly embraced the idea saying:

The proposal to include a specific date at which time all aircraft must meet or better the noise levels of FAR Part 36 is an absolutely essential component of any noise abatement plan. Progress in noise reduction will be made only if specific future goals are set now, and adhered to by those Federal agencies charged with the responsibility of reducing aircraft noise.[36]

In a communication dated September 15, 1972, American Airlines presented the following statements to the Committee:

The cost of retrofit, even within the minimum time limits that we consider achievable, is beyond the capability of the airline industry to support, and would require public funding. The January 1, 1976 date is not feasible. The earliest achievable date in our opinion is January 1, 1978.[37]

Trans World Airlines presented essentially the same view. The airlines have sought to postpone implementation of a retrofit program as long as possible, and argued that in the event it is forced upon them, the federal government must bear the cost. This amounts to saying that the taxpayers of Watts, who derive no economic benefit from the operation of Los Angeles International Airport, should pay for the cost of abating the noise to which they are subjected.

The airlines have contributed almost nothing to noise suppression research and development costs. This work has been funded by the federal government and the aircraft and engine manufacturers. The only equitable method of financing a retrofit program is to pass the cost on to the air transportation user. This could be done in either of two ways. The airlines could be made to finance the retrofit program directly, in which case the cost would be passed on to the customer. An alternative would be for the federal government to levy say a $1.00 head tax on airline passengers and place the revenue in a trust fund. In 1970, a $1.00 head tax in the United States would have generated $170 million. About $1.7 billion could be borrowed against this revenue and used to finance a retrofit program. Annual revenues from the head tax would be used to retire the loan obligation.

A final observation on the retrofitting question is in order at this point. Thus far, at least, retirement of the older, noisy four-engine aircraft from the U.S. commercial air carrier fleet has not meant these aircraft were scrapped. Usually they have been sold to other carriers. For example, in 1972 Continental Airlines sold eight DC-9-10 airplanes to Air Canada and nine Boeing 707-320Cs to five customers throughout the world. Present estimates indicate that by 1975, only about 200 of the approximately 3,500 aircraft in the world jet fleet will have been removed from service.

Annex 16 to the Convention on International Civil Aviation sets noise standards (which are almost identical to the FAR Part 36 standards) for new subsonic jet aircraft only. These standards are applicable to aircraft for which application for a type certificate was filed on or after January 1, 1969 or for aircraft with high by-pass ratio engines for which an individual certificate was issued on or after March 1, 1972. Boeing 747s manufactured after March 1, 1972 are covered by this provision. Since Canada is a member nation of ICAO, the Canadian government is expected to adopt Annex 16. However, Annex 16 contains no provisions for noise reductions in older aircraft. While ICAO is presently considering this problem, no recommendations appear likely before 1974. If, therefore, Canada and other nations seriously want to reduce the noise levels of older aircraft by 1976, they will almost certainly have to set noise limits for such aircraft and implement a retrofit program.[4]

Finally, and this is most important, technological "fixes," in general, do not provide solutions, they merely buy time, and this, usually at a price. All segments of society must recognize that the phenomenal growth which has characterized air transportation since the end of World War II simply cannot continue. In Table 6-6 we have tabulated the number of revenue passengers, revenue passenger-miles, and air carrier operations for the certificated U.S. air carriers in scheduled service for the years 1960-71. Also tabulated are total aircraft operations, which include both air carrier and general aviation operations, at airports with FAA air traffic control towers. (An aircraft operation is defined as a take-off or landing). The table shows that revenue passenger miles increased from 38.9 billion in 1960 to 135.7 billion in 1971. The annual rate of increase during this time period averaged 12 percent—a growth rate which results in a doubling of revenue passenger miles every six years.

111

Table 6-6
Revenue Passengers, Revenue Passenger-Miles, Revenue Passenger Load Factor, and Air Carrier Operations for the Certificated U.S. Air Carriers in Scheduled Service, and Total Aircraft Operations at Airports with FAA Air Traffic Control Towers

Year	Rev. Passengers (Millions of Enplanements)	Revenue Passenger-miles (Billions)	Rev. Passenger Load Factor (%)	Air Carrier Operations[1] (Millions)	Total Aircraft Operations[2] (Millions)
1960	62.256	38.863	59.3	7.706	25.774
1961	63.012	39.831	55.4	7.501	26.301
1962	67.817	43.760	53.0	7.320	28.201
1963	77.403	50.362	53.1	7.577	30.977
1964	88.520	58.494	55.0	7.909	34.195
1965	102.920	68.676	55.2	8.395	37.871
1966	118.061	79.889	58.0	8.747	44.953
1967	142.499	98.747	56.5	9.892	49.887
1968	162.181	113.958	52.6	10.696	55.292
1969	171.898	125.420	50.0	10.757	56.232
1970	169.668	131.719	49.7	10.203	55.280
1971	174.	135.652	48.5		

Sources: HANDBOOK OF AIRLINE STATISTICS, 1971 ed., Bureau of Accounts and Statistics, U.S. Civil Aeronautics Board, Washington, D.C. (1972); FAA STATISTICAL HANDBOOK OF AVIATION, 1970 ed., FAA, Dept. of Transportation, Washington, D.C. (1970); FAA AIR TRAFFIC, 1971, FAA, Dept. of Transportation, Washington, D.C. (February, 1972); U.S. STATISTICAL ABSTRACT, 1972, Census Bureau, U.S. Dept. of Commerce, Washington, D.C. (1972).

[1] An aircraft operation is defined as a take-off or landing. Air carrier operations tabulated in this column refer only to revenue operations performed in scheduled service by the certificated U.S. route air carriers.

[2] An aircraft operation is defined as a take-off or landing. Total aircraft operations tabulated in this column refer to total operations (itinerant and local) made by all aircraft (air carrier, general aviation, and military) at airports with FAA airport traffic control towers. Local operations are performed by aircraft which operate in the local traffic pattern or within sight of the tower; are known to be departing for, or arriving from, flight in local practice areas; execute simulated approaches. All aircraft arrivals or departures other than local are classified as itinerant. On January 1, 1971, there were 346 FAA-operated airport traffic control towers in the U.S.

Statistics for Canadian air carriers are given in Table 6-7. The data tabulated in columns (2)-(5) include both scheduled and charter/contract services of Group I-IV Canadian commercial air carriers. (See footnotes at the end of Table 6-7.) However, scheduled services of Air Canada, Canadian Pacific Airlines, and the five regional carriers accounted for 83 percent of the total revenue passenger miles flown by all carriers in scheduled and nonscheduled services in 1971.

Average annual rates of increase in passenger enplanements, passenger miles,

Table 6-7

Operating Statistics of Canadian Air Carriers, Groups I-IV, and Total Aircraft Operations at Airports with Department of Transport Air Traffic Control Towers, 1960-71[1]

(1) Year	(2) Revenue Passengers[2] (Millions)	(3) Revenue Passenger-miles[2] (Billions)	(4) Air Carrier Operations[2,3] (Millions)	(5) Turbine Fuel Consumed[2] (Million Gal.)	(6) Rev. Passenger Load Factor[5] (%)	(7) Total Aircraft Operations[3,4] (Millions)
1960	4.727			83.1		2.838
1961	4.951			143.8		2.446
1962	5.269			171.1		2.282
1963	5.427		0.979	187.2		2.299
1964	5.782	4.409	0.997	195.3		2.289
1965	6.570	5.196	1.104	222.3		2.688
1966	7.462	6.000	1.242	262.5		3.317
1967	8.948	7.327	1.360	316.5	62.5	4.038
1968	9.305	8.170	1.562	366.3	62.2	4.048
1969	10.264	9.484		417.5	55.6	4.326
1970	11.758	11.551	1.640	490.9	55.0	4.375
1971	12.484	11.503	1.734	501.2	56.0	

Sources: CANADA YEAR BOOK, 1965, 1968, 1970-71, Statistics Canada, Ottawa; AVIATION IN CANADA, 1971, Statistics Canada, Ottawa (February 1972); AIR CARRIER OPERATIONS IN CANADA, OCTOBER-DECEMBER, 1970 and OCTOBER-DECEMBER, 1971, Statistics Canada, Ottawa.

[1] Canadian commercial air carriers are divided into five groups as follows:

Group I: Air Canada and Canadian Pacific Airlines.
Group II: Regional air carriers. In 1971 there were 5 regional carriers: Eastern Provincial Airways, Nordair, Pacific Western Airlines, Quebecair, and Transair.

Group III: All air carriers not in Group I or II which have reported more than $500,000 gross revenue per year for combined unit toll and charter transportation, or which have reported more than $150,000 annually for unit toll revenues. In 1971 there were 39 carriers in this group.

Group IV: All air carriers reporting more than $150,000 gross annual flying revenue but not qualifying for Group III. In 1971 there were 77 carriers in this group.

Group V: All air carriers reporting less than $150,000 gross annual flying revenue. In 1971 there were 376 carriers in Group V. However, they account for less than 3% of the total operating revenues of Canadian commercial air services and less than 1% of the total ton miles.

[2] Data presented in columns (2)-(5) include both unit toll and charter/contract services of Group I-IV Canadian commercial air carriers in domestic and international operations.

Unit Toll Service is defined as the transportation of persons and/or goods between designated points at a price per passenger per mile or per pound per mile.

Charter Service is defined as the transportation of persons and/or goods from a designated base at a toll per mile or per hour for the hire of part or all of the capacity of the aircraft. Specialty flying, which consists of activities such as sightseeing, aerial photography and flying training and does not involve the transportation of persons or goods from one point to another, is not included in Charter/Contract services. Scheduled service of Air Canada, CP Air, and the 5 regional carriers accounted for 83% of the total passenger miles flown by all carriers in 1971.

[3] An aircraft operation is defined as a take-off or landing.

[4] Total aircraft operations include itinerant and local operations of air carrier and general aviation aircraft at airports with Department of Transport air traffic control towers. In 1966 there were 33 DOT tower-controlled airports in Canada. By the end of 1970, there were 47. A local operation is performed by an aircraft that operates in the local tower control zone. Aircraft that enter or leave the local tower control zone are classified as itinerant operations.

[5] Revenue Passenger Load Factor applies to scheduled service only of Canadian air carriers in Groups I-IV.

air carrier operations, and total aircraft operations for both the U.S. and Canada are given in Table 6-8. From these three tables one can readily see that while the absolute numbers in each of these categories are much smaller for Canada than for the United States, the growth rates are comparable. Should these growth rates for air travel in Canada be sustained, by 1989, revenue passenger miles flown by Canadian carriers would equal the 1971 figures for the United States! The implications of these growth rates can be illustrated in another way. Itinerant aircraft operations at Toronto International Airport increased from 99,958 in 1965 to 176,611 in 1970. If this rate of increase should continue, in 1979 the itinerant traffic at Toronto International will equal the itinerant traffic at Los Angeles International Airport during 1971—a situation unlikely to be welcomed in all segments of metropolitan Toronto.[38,39]

Whether these growth rates in air transportation will persist for some time is, of course, a bit difficult to estimate. In estimates made for U.S. air carriers in 1970, the FAA assumed that during the decade of the 1970s the annual growth rate of revenue passenger miles would be about 12 percent compared to about 14 percent during the 1960s as a result of less economic expansion, increases in air fares, and an end to the Vietnam War. The FAA has also assumed that air carrier operations will expand more slowly as the new wide-bodied jets come into service. To be sure, the slowing of economic growth which began in late 1969 is reflected in traffic statistics for 1970 and 1971. However, preliminary traffic data for the first nine months of 1972 suggest that the markedly lower growth rates in air transportation recorded in 1970 and 1971 may be only a temporary perturbation.

Some of these factors are applicable to the growth of air traffic in Canada, but there are also some additional factors. In part, this growth will depend on what policy the government adopts with regard to northern expansion. Should the government pursue a policy of northern expansion, air traffic can be expected to grow more rapidly than the above projections would indicate.

Table 6-8
Average Annual Growth Rates for Aviation in the U.S. and Canada

| | Rate of Increase (in percentage)[1] | | | |
	Revenue Passengers	Revenue Passenger-Miles	Air Carrier Operations	Total Aircraft Operations
U.S.	9.79 (1960-71)	12.04 (1960-71)	2.85 (1960-70)	7.93 (1960-70)
Canada	9.23 (1960-71)	14.68 (1964-71)	7.41 (1963-71)	4.42 (1960-70)

[1]Figures in parentheses indicate the time period over which the growth rate was calculated. Calculations are based on the data in Tables 6-6 and 6-7.

Furthermore, one must recognize that 105 of the 139 jet aircraft in the Canadian commercial air carrier fleet on July 1, 1972 were operated by Canada's two mainline carriers, Air Canada and CP Air. Most of the aircraft operated by the regional and feeder airlines are piston and turbo-prop planes. If the experience of the United States is any guide, as the number of passengers or cargo tonnage increases, these will be replaced by short- or medium-range jet aircraft (Boeing 727, Boeing 737, and DC-9), and in fact, all five of the Canadian regional carriers (Eastern Provincial, Nordair, Pacific Western, Quebecair, and Transair) have purchased such aircraft since 1968. One result will be a further increase in noise levels around existing jetports and the introduction of jet noise to a large number of communities which have never previously experienced it. If the above projections seem slightly incredible, one must remember that prior to World War II, commercial aviation was in its infancy in the United States. The present aircraft noise problem has developed almost entirely in the past twenty-five years. Thus the fact that the number of aircraft operations per year is much lower in Canada than in the United States is no cause for complacency among Canadians.

Studies of the subjective response of people to aircraft noise have shown that doubling the number of flyovers is equivalent to a 3-4 PNdB increase in the noise level for each flyover. The importance of this factor in relation to air traffic growth is graphically illustrated by the increase in jet aircraft operations in Canada in recent years. Itinerant jet aircraft operations at Canadian airports with DOT air traffic control towers increased from 106,000 in 1965 to 441,000 in 1970. (See footnotes to Table 6-7 for definition of itinerant operations.) If this rate of increase should continue for the remainder of this decade, itinerant jet aircraft operations would reach 7.6 million in 1980—a seventeenfold increase over the 1970 level. Just to offset the increased volume of jet traffic, each aircraft would have to be approximately 15 EPNdB quieter than those in service today. While the new DC-10 and L-1011 are about 15 EPNdB quieter on both take-off and landing than the noisy B-707 and DC-8 aircraft, they are only about 5 EPNdB quieter than existing B-727, B-737, and DC-9 aircraft (see Figures 6-9 and 6-10). Note also, that the noise reductions that would result from a retrofit program for these aircraft, as shown in Table 6-2, are not sufficient to offset such traffic growth. We can therefore conclude with reasonable certainty, that if the growth in jet traffic which has characterized the past several years continues, its effects will not be offset by technological improvements during the remainder of this decade and a further deterioration in the noise environment will occur.

In addition to the increasing number of take-offs and landings at established airports, the growth in air traffic volume is causing a proliferation of airports in major metropolitan regions. Regional airports, such as the new one under construction for Dallas-Fort Worth, if properly located and used as the *only* jetport for the region, can result in greatly reduced noise levels in existing cities. Unfortunately, construction of a new metropolitan airport has rarely resulted in abandonment of the old one. Chicago is now searching for a site for a second regional airport; a major controversy surrounds the selection of a site for a third major airport for London; and New York City is looking for a place to build a fourth airport to serve the New York City area. The Los Angeles metropolitan area, well known for its endless rows of tract houses and sprawling freeway network, is presently served by four major airports: Los Angeles International, Ontario, Hollywood-Burbank, and Long Beach. As part of a plan that appears little short of a blueprint for disaster, the Los Angeles Department of Airports has begun acquisition of 17,000 acres near Palmdale, 60 miles northeast of the city, for a new airport. A large airport requires a large service staff, and, in fact, the Department of Airports has estimated that the Palmdale airport, when operational, will employ 35,000 people. Because of the 60 miles separating the city from the airport—a distance which will be spanned only by freeway—a large percentage of these employees can be expected to live in the Palmdale area. The ultimate result, of course, will be an airport surrounded by a city and a recurrence of all the noise problems associated with existing LAX. Even worse is the fact that V/STOL (Vertical or Short Takeoff and Landing aircraft) service is planned between the five airports and more than two dozen points in the metropolitan area. If all such flight paths are superimposed on a map of the Los Angeles area, one finds that very nearly all of Los Angeles County, an area of 4,080 square miles, will be subjected to aircraft flyover noise in excess of 90 PNdB on the ground.[40]

If any semblance of a sane environment is to be maintained, a reduction in the growth rate of air traffic is imperative. Such a proposal seems unlikely to receive a warm reception from the airlines who can be expected to claim they are merely satisfying a public demand. But are they, or are they in reality creating a demand to fulfill? In 1971, for example, the 39 certificated U.S. air carriers spent $1.15 billion on promotion and sales.[34]

A reduction in the growth rate of air traffic or, in fact, an actual reduction in traffic should not be as difficult to achieve as one may at first suppose. Table 6-6 gives the revenue passenger load factor for the certificated U.S. air carriers in scheduled service for the period 1960-71. The highest load factor recorded was 59.3 percent in 1960, and since 1966, load factors have steadily declined. Since the break-even load factor for the carriers as a group was 47.9 percent in 1970, air carrier operations showed a small profit for the year even though half the total seats flown were empty. (Several of the individual trunk carriers did sustain large operating losses in 1970 and 1971.) Even in 1966, however, which was the most profitable year U.S. air carriers have ever enjoyed, nearly half the total seats flown were empty. A good case can be made for the existence of far too much competition in an industry which, ironically, is heavily government regulated. The Civil Aeronautics Board (CAB) sets fares, establishes route structures, and has final authority on airline mergers. But is the public really well served by a system which, for example, allows seven carriers to operate in the

Mainland-Hawaii market when, in fact, all of them are losing money on the operation because of poor load factors.

A major reappraisal of the route structure is in order, and noise reduction should be an important consideration in such deliberations. If mergers between carriers were encouraged, adequate service could be maintained with far fewer flights and higher load factors than we have today. Unfortunately, the CAB seems considerably more interested in promoting aviation than in promoting quiet. Early in 1972, the CAB refused to even hold a hearing on a petition filed by the City of Inglewood (which adjoins Los Angeles International Airport) in which the city requested decertification of one carrier serving Los Angeles International. Inglewood maintained that decertification would reduce air traffic volume while simultaneously improving load factors on other flights.[41] Apparently the CAB still believes exponential growth can somehow be made permanent. It can't.

Some economists have suggested that one possible solution would be to allow the carriers to operate in a free market economy without interference by the CAB. In such a situation, the carriers would almost certainly cut fares instead of reducing the seating capacity of their aircraft by installation of lounges and piano bars or resorting to other gimmicks to attract passengers. In the ensuing economic struggle, unprofitable routes would be abandoned, and the less efficient carriers would not survive and would be forced into mergers. The net result would be a reduction in both the number of carriers and the number of routes operated. Regardless of the method used to attain it, this is obviously the goal toward which we should be striving.

In western Europe the situation is quite different. Since the major European carriers are government subsidized, most nations have only one major carrier. Perhaps flights are not as frequent as some travelers would like, but to what extent must the well-being of whole cities be sacrificed for the convenience of those who travel by air?

The present situation in Canada lies somewhere in between. Regulation of civil aviation in Canada falls within the jurisdiction of the federal government under the terms of the Aeronautics Act and the National Transportation Act (SC 1967, c.69). The Aeronautics Act is divided into three parts. Part I, which deals with the registration of aircraft, licensing of pilots, maintenance of airports and air navigation facilities, accident investigation, and aircraft operations, is administered by the Air Services Branch, Ministry of Transport. Its functions are comparable to those of the FAA in the United States. Part II is concerned with the economic aspects of commercial air services, and it assigns to the Canadian Transport Commission authority to license all commercial air services in Canada and to regulate routes, fares, and all other economic matters. The Canadian Transport Commission was organized on September 19, 1967 under the provisions of the National Transportation Act. In order to function, the Commission has established a number of Committees, any of which may exercise the powers of the Commission. The Air Transport Committee controls commercial air services in Canada.[38,42,43]

In formulating its aviation policy in 1964, the Canadian government adopted the principle that competition on domestic services should not seriously injure Air Canada's economic viability in the domestic market. The Minister of Transport defined somewhat more precisely the respective areas of operation for Air Canada and Canadian Pacific Airlines. Subsequently, the Canadian Transport Commission authorized CP Air to operate transcontinental service and to serve Calgary, Edmonton, and Ottawa. In its 1964 policy, the government also recommended that the regional carriers be given greater scope in route development including, where appropriate, limited competition on mainline route segments of Air Canada's or CP Air's route system. According to a recent report, *Aviation in Canada, 1971*, published by the Transportation and Public Utilities Division of Statistics Canada:

In general, the various boards and the Air Transport Committee of the CTC have adhered to the principle of "regulated competition," allowing two airlines to serve the same route only when it appeared economically feasible to do so.

The situation is by no means out of hand, but it merits careful watching, for the airline industry can exert enormous pressures for route expansion. As the situation in the United States so clearly demonstrates, the criterion of economic viability will allow a very much higher level of competition than is desirable from the standpoint of noise reduction. In fact, the data in column 6 of Table 6-7 suggest this may have already occurred. Revenue passenger load factors for Canadian air carriers in scheduled service dropped from 62.5 percent in 1966 to 55.6 percent in 1968 and remained at about that level in 1969 and 1970.

A related area in which government has a vital role to play is in the development of high-speed rail transportation for short-haul distances under 400 miles. The Boston-New York and Washington-New York routes, in that order, rank as the two largest domestic air passenger markets in the United States. Since the intercity rail distance on each route is less than 230 miles, efficient, high-speed rail transportation could significantly reduce aircraft flyovers in this densely populated northeast corridor. Other important air markets in the northeast corridor presently include Boston-Washington, Boston-Philadelphia, Baltimore-New York, Hartford-New York, Philadelphia-Washington and Philadelphia-New York. In 1968, 36 percent of all U.S. domestic air passenger originations took place at fifteen cities in the northeast corridor. Of the 54 million air passengers that originated at these fifteen cities, more than 18 million or 34 percent were intra-northeast corridor passengers. A very large percentage of these 18 million air passengers could presumably be enticed to choose rail transit.[44]

In early 1969 preliminary high-speed rail demonstration programs, joint projects of the federal government and Penn Central Railroad, were inaugurated in the Washington-New York and Boston-New York markets. If the programs are successful, full-scale operating systems incorporating faster, more confortable, and more convenient rail service may follow. The trains have controlled heating and air conditioning, special acoustical treatment, indirect lighting, carpeting, snack bar service, at-seat food service in parlor cars, and telephone service. A number of operating characteristics and features of the projects are given in Table 6-9. Service on the New York-Washington route was inaugurated on January 16, 1969, with one round-trip Metroliner per day. As shown by the data in Table 6-10, business grew steadily during the year as schedules were increased to three round trips per day (including one nonstop) for about nine months and finally to six round trips during the last three months of the year. The Metroliner has a distinct price advantage over air transportation ($15.60 vs. $23.10 air shuttle) and offers essentially identical traveling time from city center to city center.

The effect which introduction of Metroliner service in 1969 has had on air and rail passenger travel between Washington and New York is reflected by the data in Table 6-11. Air passengers remained almost constant at the 1968 level while the number of rail passengers increased 44 percent, reversing a long downward trend in rail passenger travel. Metroliner service accounted for 238,800 of the 731,200 rail passengers for the New York-Washington city pair in 1969. These results appear even more remarkable when one considers that for most of the first nine months of the year only three daily round-trip Metroliners were operated while the airlines offer more than fifty daily round trips between Washington and New York.

Public reception of the Metroliner service has been encouraging, as the data in Tables 6-12 and 6-13 show. Table 6-12 presents a comparison of train passengers' ratings of service attributes on conventional passenger trains and on Metroliner service in the New York-Washington corridor. We see that in nearly every category the Metroliner scored a major improvement in passenger rating. Particularly significant is the fact that 93 percent of Metroliner passengers gave a good-excellent rating to the category of overall pleasant experience while only 59 percent of passengers rated conventional trains good-excellent in this category.

Table 6-13 presents a comparison of past and anticipated travel modes between passengers on conventional trains and Metroliner passengers. Especially significant is the fact that 23 percent of Metroliner passengers said they used air transportation the last time, but only 7 percent said they intend to use air transportation the next time.

In summary, we see that noise from aircraft, both air carrier and general aviation, is a serious and exceedingly widespread problem, and unless current trends are reversed, the situation is destined to become very much worse. Since there is no single panacea for the problem on the horizon, reversal of these trends and alleviation of the present intolerable noise levels in some communities

Table 6-9
Facts on High-Speed Rail Demonstration Projects[4][5]

Characteristics	Boston – New York	Washington – New York
Name of trains	Turbos I and II	Metroliner
Length of longest run	229 miles	226 miles
Speed	Max. capability of 160 mph.	Max. capability of 160 mph.
Frequency	One round trip daily	Six round trips daily
Time	3 hours 40 minutes Standard rail service: 4½ hours Total air travel time: 2½ hours[1]	2½ hours Standard rail service: 4 hours Total air travel time: 2½ hours[1]
Fares	$13.75 one way compared with $11.58 in conventional trains. Air shuttle fare: $21.00	$15.75 one way compared with $11.75 in conventional trains. Air Shuttle fare: $23.10
Participants	Federal Govt., Penn Central Railroad, and United Aircraft Corp.	Federal Govt. and Penn Central Railroad
Cost of project	Government: $9 million	Government: $13 million Penn Central: $58 million
Off-train features	Improvement of existing track; simplified reservation and ticketing systems	Baggage conveyor system; new platforms in Washington, Baltimore, and Wilmington, Del.; two new suburban stations in Md. and N.J.
On-train features	Wide range of prepared foods served from modern facilities; fast acceleration and braking; new suspension design to give greater comfort on curves; dome observation sections; electric heating and air conditioning.	Indirect lighting; special acoustical treatment; carpeting; snack bar service in parlor cars; telephone service; specially designed reclining seats; controlled heating and air conditioning systems.

[1]Travel time to and from airports: 70 minutes; scheduled jet flight time: 50 minutes; delays due to congestion at New York City airports: 30 minutes (Northeast Airlines reports that air traffic delays at New York City airports now average 30 minutes between 4 and 8 P.M.).

Table 6-10
New York-Washington City Pair Rail Passengers in Both Directions, Calendar Year 1969[4][5]

Month	Metroliner	Conventional	Total
January[1]	3,700	45,200	48,900
February	11,100	47,100	58,200
March	15,400	36,500	51,900
April	22,000	45,300	67,300
May	20,800	42,500	63,300
June	22,400	47,600	70,000
July	21,000	46,000	67,000
August	21,000	50,000	71,000
September	17,500	33,400	50,900
October	20,600	31,300	51,900
November	30,400	34,600	65,000
December	32,900	32,900	65,800
Totals	238,800	492,400	731,200

[1]Metroliner service started January 16, 1969.

Table 6-11
New York-Washington City Pair Passengers in Both Directions, 1960-1969[4][5]

Calendar Year	Air	Rail
1960	726,000	858,000
1966	1,510,000	648,000
1967	1,842,000	546,000
1968	1,901,000	509,000
1969	1,909,000	731,000

will require a coordinated approach to the problem and positive governmental action. While the technical problems are formidable, the economic ones seem more so. The basic difficulty here stems from the fact that the powerful air transport industry espouses the philosophy that unlimited growth is a necessary and desirable goal. Because increases in air fares might tend to dampen this growth, the industry generally opposes any expenditures which would have to be passed on to airline customers in the form of fare increases. Therefore, as long as the air transportation industry is governed only by market place economics, there will be no reductions in aircraft noise. For this reason a good case can be made for placing the responsibility for aircraft noise abatement in a separate

Table 6-12

Passengers' Ratings of Service Attributes on Metroliner and Conventional Trains in the New York-Washington Corridor[4][6]

Service Attributes	Metroliner Passenger Ratings[1]		Conventional Train Passenger Ratings[1]	
	Excellent-Good	Fair-Poor	Excellent-Good	Fair-Poor
Comfort of seats	97%	3%	58%	42%
Quietness	81	19	50	50
Smoothness	55	45	46	54
Lighting	98	2	72	28
Temperature	85	15	54	46
Cleanliness	99	1	38	62
Attractiveness	97	3	28	72
Courtesy of conductor	96	4	90	10
Time trip took	92	8	77	23
Cost of train	85	15	70	30
Overall pleasant experience	93	7	59	41
The food	64	36	38	62

[1] Passenger opinion was sampled in on-train surveys conducted during the period January-June 1969.

Table 6-13

Past and Anticipated Travel Mode Usage Among Rail Passengers in the New York-Washington Corridor[4][6]

Mode	Mode Used Last Time[1]		Mode Expected to be Used Next Time[1]	
	Conventional Train Passengers	Metroliner Passengers	Conventional Train Passengers	Metroliner Passengers
Train	71%	50%	82%	84%
Bus	4	4	2	1
Auto	19	23	12	8
Plane	6	23	4	7
Totals	100%	100%	100%	100%

[1] On-train passenger surveys conducted during the period January-June 1969 among rail passengers in the New York-Washington corridor.

office of noise abatement or in the federal department or ministry of health and welfare. In the United States, Canada, and most nations of western Europe, this responsibility is presently vested in the respective departments of transportation which seem to be considerably more interested in promoting aviation rather than regulating it. Sweden presents something of a contrast in this regard. While the Royal Board of Civil Aviation controls all air traffic, local health authorities have the responsibility to prevent "sanitary nuisance." In late 1968 the Civil Aviation Board authorized the use of DC-9 jets at Bromma Airport, three miles from the center of Stockholm. Stockholm health authorities applied to the federal government, claiming that a sanitary nuisance would affect thousands of people. The response of the federal government was to prohibit the use of jets at Bromma for an indefinite time.

Divesting the FAA of its authority for aircraft noise control and placing this responsibility in the Environmental Protection Agency (EPA) appears to be a mandatory prerequisite for effective abatement of aircraft noise in the United States. Unfortunately, the Noise Control Act of 1972 (P.L. 92-574) places EPA in the role of a mere consultant to the FAA in the promulgation of aircraft noise standards and leaves the final authority with the FAA. This is a very serious weakness of the Act, and unless this provision is changed, any significant abatement of aircraft noise appears highly unlikely. In a minority report on the bill from the Senate Public Works Committee, Senator Edmund Muskie observed:

To date, regulation of aircraft noise pollution has been the sole responsibility of the Federal Aviation Administration. The Federal Aviation Administration has had this responsibility since its inception. It has had a specific legislative mandate for the past four years. And its record is wholly inadequate.

I understand why the Federal Aviation Administration's response has been inadequate. The FAA's responsibility is not to reduce the environmental impact caused by aircraft noise. Its primary responsibility is to promote air commerce and to protect safety. Regulation of noise from aircraft is not consistent with that primary mission.

The attitude of the Federal Aviation Administration as regards regulation of aircraft noise was more clearly spelled out in the following excerpt from a draft report on noise pollution prepared by the Environmental Protection Agency:

"Both directly and by unmistakable inference, a number of important conclusions arise from the information gathered on federal noise control programs.

"Most plainly, the control of unwanted sound is not a high priority issue for virtually any Federal agency or department. Only when an Agency's primary mission absolutely requires a commitment of time, manpower, and funding to noise control to assure smooth functioning of that primary mission (as with for instance, FAA and NASA) is even a modest venture into noise suppression undertaken. For the FAA, aircraft noise is only an annoying interference in the basic goal of the Agency: the most efficient, safest, and swiftest air travel possible."

Continuation of the Federal Aviation Administration in a role of determining the degree to which noise emissions from aircraft will be reduced is not justified by the record.[47]

The Supersonic Transport and Sonic Boom

Regardless of how insufferable people find today's noise levels, the worst is yet to come when—and if—the supersonic transport (SST) enters commercial airline service sometime in the mid-1970s. Three commercial supersonic transports are under development. A joint British-French effort is producing the Concorde, which has already undergone supersonic test flights both over Britain and between Britain and Dakar in West Africa. The Soviet Union conducted the first supersonic test flight of its TU-144 in June of 1969. In the United States, the Boeing Company, with the help of federal funding, was developing the U.S. entry into the SST market, the Boeing 2707-300. Table 6-14 gives a comparative summary of data for the three airplanes as of June 1971. Some of the figures in the table, such as sale price, change with time.

In December of 1970, however, the SST ran head on into the new ethic of ecology and in an historic vote the U.S. Senate voted 52 to 41 to withhold a $290 million appropriation for construction of two prototypes of the Boeing 2707-300. Since the House of Representatives had already approved the appropriation, the measure went to a joint Senate-House conference committee from which a compromise emerged which allowed interim financing of the program through March of 1971. When the appropriation again came before Congress in March of 1971, both the House of Representatives and the Senate rejected the appropriation bill. However, in May, partly because of rising unemployment and partly because of some intense lobbying by plane supporters, the House reversed itself and voted 201-195 to appropriate $85.3 million for continued development work. At a Washington press conference after the vote, Boeing chairman William Allen said that Congress would have to appropriate $500 million to $1 billion before the company would be interested in restarting the program. Furthermore, he indicated that public funding would be required right up until the time planes were delivered to the carriers. Throughout the congressional debate, the plane's supporters had been saying that the federal government was being asked only to fund two prototypes. But Allen stated, "The Boeing Company never said that."

The House victory was a short-lived one, and on May 19, 1971 the U.S. Senate killed the appropriation by a vote of 58-37. A number of factors, including the cost to the taxpayer, the economics of SST operation, concern over the environmental consequences, and questions about the nation's priorities were all responsible for the defeat of the SST. Sen. William Proxmire (D., Wisc.) observed:

On this SST project we are asked to spend $290 million to increase air pollution. This year we will spend only $208 million for mass transportation to provide the opportunity for literally millions of people to get to work. But we are going to spend $290 million here to provide a relatively small portion of the American people the means to fly overseas more rapidly. That does not make sense.[1]

Table 6-14
Comparison of SST Data*

	Boeing 2707-300	Concorde	TU-144
Maximum gross weight	750,000 lbs.	385,000 lbs.	330,000 lbs.
Material	Titanium	Aluminum	Aluminum
Length	289 feet	193 feet	188½ feet
Height	55 feet	38 feet	34½ feet
Engines	4 - GE4/J6G	4 - Bristol-Siddley Olympus 593	4 - Kuznetzov NK-144
Thrust (augmented) per engine	67,800 lbs.	38,300 lbs.	38,500 lbs.
Passengers	298	128	120
Payload	60,200 lbs.	28,000 lbs.	26,000 lbs.
Take-off distance	10,540 feet	10,900 feet	1[1]
Landing distance	8,250 feet	8,200 feet	1[1]
Landing approach speed	177 miles per hr.	185 miles per hr.	182 miles per hr.
Cruise speed	Mach 2.7 (1,786 mph)	Mach 2.05 (1,350 mph)	Mach 2.35 (1,550 mph)
Ave. cruise altitude	63,000 feet	56,000 feet	59,000 feet
First flight	–	March 2, 1969	Dec. 31, 1968
First supersonic flight	–	October, 1969	June, 1969
First airline service	–	1974	1974
Sales reservations, U.S.	–	38	0
Sales reservations, other than U.S.	–	74	1[1]
Sales price	$37,000,000	$26,000,000	1[1]

*As of June 1971. Some of the figures in the table, such as sales prices, delivery positions, etc. are subject to change with time.
[1] Unknown.

Whether the plane is dead or merely in limbo for a while is a question open to some debate. Apparently hoping that international competition will revive the SST, the Transportation Department, NASA, and the Boeing Company have continued a small research effort. In a front-page story on November 1, 1972, the *Wall Street Journal* observed, "Die-hard supporters of the project, still refusing to admit defeat, are beginning to try to resurrect the supposed corpse." These supporters include Boeing's present board chairman, T.A. Wilson, former SST program director William Magruder, Federal Aviation Administrator John Shaffer, and President Nixon's domestic affairs advisor John Ehrlichman. Ehrlichman told a Seattle group that start-up money for the SST might be included in the fiscal year 1974 budget. The Administration's budget for fiscal year 1974, released in January 1973, does indeed contain a $42 million request for SST research and development. President Nixon inspected a Concorde prototype during a visit to the Azores in 1971 and is reported to still feel that the United States should have an entry in the SST race.[2]

William Magruder contends that if the SST program is resurrected, the government will have to finance not only prototype development, but subsequent development, production tooling, and certification of the aircraft as well. The estimated cost to the taxpayers for all this is now reported to be approximately $5.5 billion—a sum that congress may be unwilling to spend.

The environmental consequences that operation of a large fleet of SSTs would have are both numerous and serious. Some of these effects, such as the drain on the world's energy resources and the sonic boom, are reasonably predictable. The extent to which other effects, such as the possible reduction of the ozone concentration in the upper atmosphere, weather modification due to injection of particles and large masses of water into the stratosphere, and possible harm to passengers as a result of exposure to cosmic radiation, may occur is not so easy to assess in advance. The difficulty is, of course, that once a fleet of SSTs becomes operational, the economic interests involved will make an honest appraisal of such effects difficult, and abandonment of supersonic operations almost impossible.

Our concern here is with the noise that supersonic aircraft generate, and there are two aspects of the noise problem. One is the conventional jet noise produced by the engines; the other is the so-called sonic boom, which we will consider first.

Whenever an airplane flies faster than the speed of sound (344 meters/sec. or 770 mph at sea level and about 660 mph at 70,000 feet), it generates shock waves at each point where the surface of the plane greatly disturbs the air. Thus, the major shock waves are generated at the front of the airplane, the leading and trailing edges of the wing, and the trailing edge of the tail. Figure 6-11 illustrates the shock waves generated by the separate components of the XB-70 supersonic bomber. The individual shock waves define what is called the "near field" pressure signature, that is the character of the pressure pulse at short distances

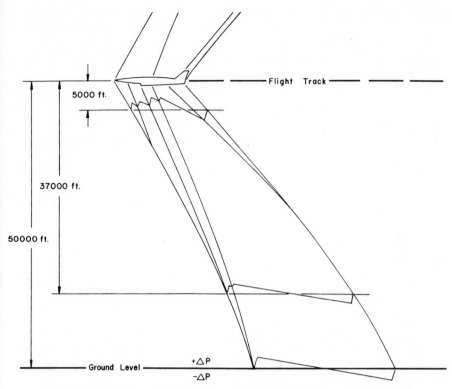

Figure 6-11. Schematic Illustration of the Shock Waves Produced by Different Parts of the XB-70 Supersonic Bomber and the Resulting Pressure Signatures Found at Various Distances from the Aircraft. Note: Notice that the individual shock waves that characterize the near-field pressure signature eventually coalesce into just two shock waves.[3]

from the aircraft. As these shock waves move through the air, they tend to coalesce into just two conical waves, a bow wave and a tail wave, which emanate from the aircraft. The resulting pressure fluctuation shown at ground level in the figure is called an "N-wave." The figure also shows that as the distance from the aircraft is increased, the distance between the bow and tail shock waves increases. Theoretically, the length of the pressure signature varies approximately as the one-quarter power of the distance from the aircraft.

When these shock waves intercept the ground, the pressure signature they produce causes the double clap we call sonic boom. These conical shock waves and the resulting pressure signatures are illustrated in Figures 6-11 and 6-12. There exists a common misconception that the boom is produced only once

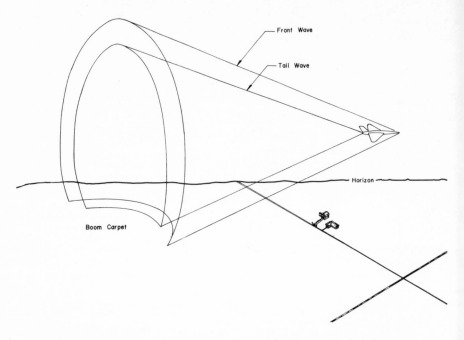

Figure 6-12. Diagram of the Conical Shock Waves Produced by a Supersonic Aircraft. Note: The area on the ground which is intersected by these shock waves receives the sonic boom and is frequently called the "boom carpet."

when the plan first exceeds the speed of sound, but in fact, the boom is produced continuously while the plane is in supersonic flight. The area on the ground which receives the shock waves is often called the boom carpet.

Sonic boom strength is usually expressed in terms of overpressure, i.e., by the magnitude of the positive vertical displacement of the N-shaped shock wave shown in Figures 6-11 and 6-13. Note, however, that the total pressure variation is actually double that of the so-called overpressure. The strength of the boom and the width of the boom carpet depend upon many factors, some of which are understood and some of which are not. Shock wave strength depends rather directly on the lift of the airplane, but since lift is a function of size and weight, boom strength increases with size and weight of the aircraft. It also increases somewhat with the speed of the plane. However, boom strength on the ground decreases as the 3/4 power of altitude of the aircraft, partly because at higher altitudes the mass of air that can be compressed by the aircraft is smaller. Shock wave strength is also dependent on other features of the aircraft such as shape, design of the leading edges, and angle of attack.

Unpredictability of boom strength has been noted in connection with operation of military aircraft at supersonic speeds for a long time, but the

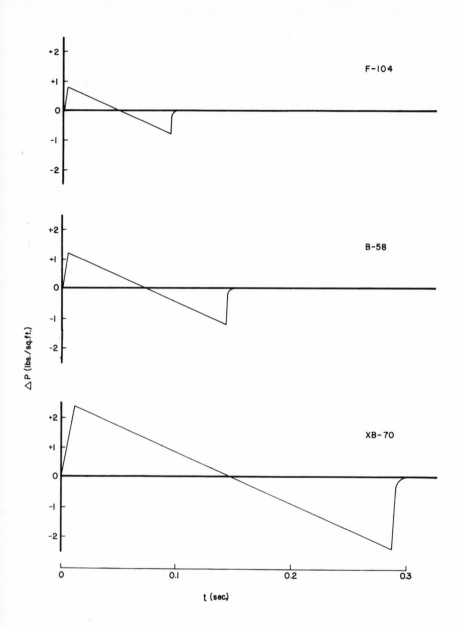

Figure 6-13. Schematic Diagram of N-Wave Pressure Signatures on the Ground Generated by Three Types of Military Aircraft Flying at a Speed of Mach 2 and an Altitude of 50,000 Ft.

Oklahoma City tests, which will be discussed shortly, demonstrated that the scatter was much greater than previously supposed. Various atmospheric conditions such as wind, turbulence, non-uniform temperature distribution such as temperature inversions, etc., are apparently responsible for these variations in boom intensity and hence for a rather high probability of magnification of the boom intensity above the nominal intensity. Such magnified boom intensities are often referred to as "superbooms."

In the Oklahoma City tests, nominal sonic boom overpressures of 1.5 and 2.0 psf were sought, but as Table 6-15 shows, the measured average values were somewhat less. Nevertheless, several measurements of 4.4 psf were recorded, and microphones placed at 200-foot intervals along the flight track revealed a fourfold variation in overpressure within an 800-foot interval during one overflight. From the Oklahoma City data Lundberg has calculated that an overpressure at least twice as strong as the nominal value will occur with a probability of 0.001 (0.1 percent of the time).[5]

Various aircraft maneuvers such as acceleration, turns, and "pushovers" (the change from climbing attitude to horizontal flight and the change from horizontal flight to descent) cause focusing of the shock waves on the ground and hence magnified boom overpressures.[6,7]

As the shock wave passes through the air its energy is gradually dissipated due to air friction, but it may travel 25 to 50 miles before the overpressure is reduced to essentially zero. Because commercial supersonic transports are much larger than most supersonic military aircraft, they are expected to produce boom carpets 50 to 80 miles wide. A profile of shock wave intensity across such a carpet is shown in Figure 6-14.[3,5,6,8,9]

The figure shows that overpressure decreases with increasing lateral distance from the flight track. Under the test conditions, the lateral cut-off, i.e., the point at which the measured overpressure declines rapidly to zero, occurs at a distance of 30 miles from the flight track. Beyond this distance the boom is not perceived.

Table 6-15

Schedule and Measured Median Sonic Boom Overpressures for the Oklahoma City Tests[4]

Study Period	Time Period	No. of Booms Daily	Nominal Overpressure (psf)	Measured Median Boom Overpressures (psf)		
				0-8 Miles	8-12 Miles	12-16 Miles
1	0-3 weeks	Gradual increase from 1 to 8	Gradual increase from 1.0 to 1.5	1.13	0.8	0.65
2	4-19 weeks	8	1.5	1.23	1.1	0.85
3	19-26 weeks	8	2.0	1.60	1.3	1.00

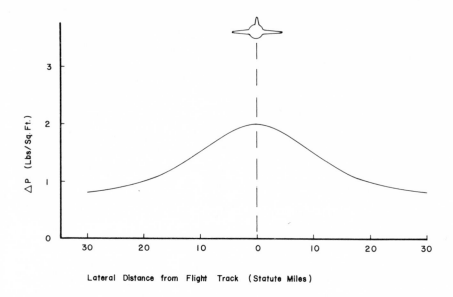

Figure 6-14. Profile of Shock Wave Intensity on the Ground Across the Sonic Boom Carpet Generated by an XB-70 Supersonic Bomber Flown at a Speed of Mach 2.0 and an Altitude of 60,000 Ft. Note: Under the test conditions, the lateral cut-off distance is about 30 miles.[3]

Duration of the sonic boom is roughly proportional to the length of the plane. Prior to 1966, the largest operational supersonic aircraft was the B-58 bomber which has a length of 97 feet, a maximum gross weight of about 160,000 pounds, and a maximum speed of about Mach 2. This airplane and various fighter aircraft were used in the 1964 Oklahoma City tests and other sonic boom flight test programs. In late 1966 the XB-70 supersonic bomber was used in sonic boom tests at Edwards Air Force Base, and in 1967 the SR-71, a high-altitude reconnaissance plane began flying supersonically across the United States. The SR-71 is slightly longer (107 ft.) but not quite as heavy (120,000 lbs.) as the B-58, and can operate at altitudes above 80,000 feet, much higher than the B-58. Comparing these figures with the data in Table 6-14 we see that even the Concorde is almost twice as long and two and one-half times as heavy as either of these aircraft. Indeed, in both length and weight, the Concorde is similar to the XB-70, which has a length of 183 feet and a maximum gross weight of about 530,000 pounds.

In Figure 6-13, the N-wave pressure signatures generated by three types of military aircraft flying at a speed of Mach 2 and an altitude of 50,000 feet are compared. Both the F-104 and B-58 were used in the Oklahoma City tests. Because of similarities in weight and size, the Concorde can be expected to have a pressure signature comparable to that for the XB-70. From Figure 6-13 we also see that the bow wave and tail wave from the F-104 arrive so close together that they are perceived as a single clap. Because of the wide separation of the two shock waves from the XB-70 and Concorde, two distinct reports separated by an interval of almost 0.3 second will be heard. If flown at low altitudes, the F-104 and B-58 are both capable of producing very high overpressures on the ground. Of course, the boom duration would decrease as the flight altitude is lowered.

In an attempt to mollify public opinion in the United States, the FAA has said that no civilian SST will be permitted to fly at supersonic speeds over the continental United States. However, the FAA has not been known for keeping its word, and Major General Jewell C. Maxwell, former chief of the SST program for the FAA, the agency which was funding the program, has said, "We believe that people in time will come to accept the sonic boom as they have the rather unpleasant side effects which have accompanied other advances in transportation."

General Maxwell's statement is in disagreement with a considerable body of scientific evidence. In an apparent attempt to gain some measure of public acceptance of sonic booms, the FAA and the U.S. Air Force have conducted a number of sonic boom experiments. Some of these tests, such as those carried out at Edwards Air Force Base, were conducted on populations comprised almost exclusively of air force personnel and hence the results are essentially meaningless. The most comprehensive and carefully controlled test on a civilian population was the one conducted in Oklahoma City over a 26-week period in 1964. A 100 mile-long flight path was established in the area and sonic booms were generated by three types of fighter aircraft and a B-58 bomber operating in the altitude range of 21,000 to 50,000 feet and speed range of Mach 1.2 to 2.0. Aircraft were positioned over the flight track by ground control radar and velocities were determined from radar tracking. Constant-velocity level flight was attained in the vicinity of Minco, Oklahoma and maintained across the test area (see Figure 6-15). Overpressures at ground level were recorded by microphones located at fixed positions directly under the flight track and at lateral distances of 5 and 10 miles from the track. In addition, a number of portable units recorded ground-level overpressures throughout the test area.[4]

The test schedule is shown in Table 6-15. During the first three weeks, the boom intensities were to be increased from 1.0 to 1.5 psf, maintained at 1.5 psf for the next fifteen weeks, and increased to 2.0 psf for the last eight weeks. Although there were wide variations in peak overpressures for individual sonic booms, Table 6-15 shows that the median overpressures measured were somewhat below the values predicted at the beginning of the tests.

Personal interviews were conducted with almost 3,000 local adult residents to determine their reactions to the booms. Each person was interviewed three different times during the course of the tests, and the results of the interviews are shown in Figure 6-16. At the conclusion of the tests, 27 percent felt they

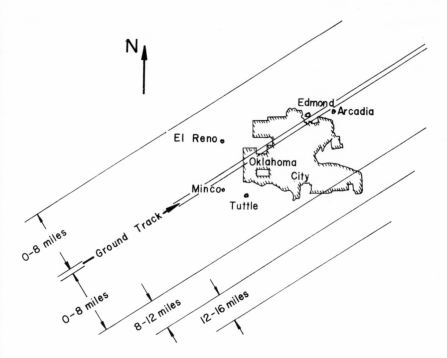

Figure 6-15. Map of the Oklahoma City Area Showing the Test Flight Track in Relation to the City. Note: Lateral distance from the flight track was divided into three different belts for the purpose of providing three different average overpressure levels for the personal interview survey.

could never learn to live with sonic booms, 56 percent reported serious annoyance, and 94 percent said the booms caused some interference in their daily lives. In addition, 4,901 residents filed damage claims against the government.[4]

There are several aspects of the Oklahoma City tests which suggest that if the results do not exhibit a definite bias, they are certainly the most favorable the FAA could hope to achieve. Nearly one-third of the population of the city is dependent upon the aviation industry for its living. Prior to the start of the tests, the FAA conducted a public information program via pamphlets and the local news media in which the nature of the tests was explained and the study was presented as a part of the U.S. SST development program. The exact flight times of the eight sonic booms generated daily were well publicized. During the test runs, the aircraft were visible to people on the ground, and no booms were generated during the night. In summary, one must concede that these conditions

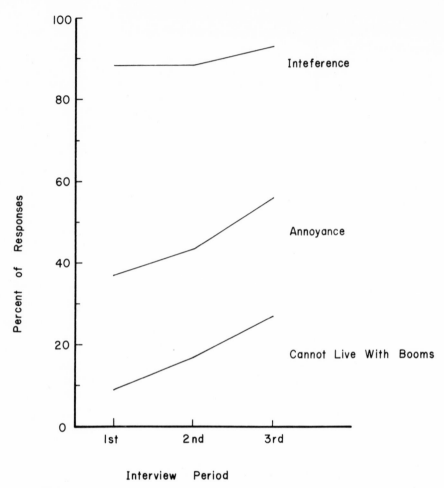

Figure 6-16. Results of the Three Series of Interviews with Nearly 3,000 Adult Residents of Oklahoma City During the 1964 Sonic Boom Tests.[4]

are rather far removed from those which would be encountered in the operation of a fleet of commercial SSTs.

Military aircraft have been flying at supersonic speeds over parts of the United States for nearly two decades. Usually, such flights have been restricted to relatively unpopulated areas, but there have been some accidental low-level incidents, and some Strategic Air Command operations were conducted over heavily populated areas (San Francisco, Chicago, Pittsburg, St. Louis, and Minneapolis to name a few). Table 6-16 shows a list of claims for sonic boom damage in the United States which have been presented to the air force since

Table 6-16
Summary of Sonic Boom Damage Claims in the U.S. Against the Air Force Since
Fiscal Year 1956[10]

Fiscal Year	No. of Claims Filed	Dollars Claimed[1]	Claims Approved in Whole or Part	Dollars Approved
1956	36	$ 12,000	21	$ 2,000
1957	372	157,000	286	19,000
1958	522	196,000	235	40,000
1959	632	285,000	243	21,000
1960	681	108,000	227	20,000
1961	1,146	703,000	527	57,000
1962	3,092	990,000[2]	1,451	132,000
1963	7,200	4,023,000	2,268	239,000
1964	5,102	3,545,000	1,664	183,000
1965	9,574	4,938,000	2,490	256,000
1966	4,856	3,284,000	2,123	211,000
1967	2,216	1,732,000	1,080	145,000
1968[3]	3,054	2,236,000	1,278	135,000
Totals	38,483	$22,209,000	13,893	$1,460,000

[1]Rounded to the nearest thousand dollars.
[2]One claim for $19 million not included.
[3]First ten months of the fiscal year only.

Fiscal Year 1956 and the disposition of those claims. The air force has a procedure for handling sonic boom damage claims. A complaint of damage may be presented in any manner to an air force claims office. The air force, upon receiving the complaint, sends the claimant forms and instructions for presenting his claim. After the claim has been received by the air force, an air force claims officer conducts or supervises an investigation into the cause of damage. The air force maintains that out of every three persons sent a claim form, only one will actually present a claim. There appear to be several reasons for this. One is that if the damage is small, the difficulties involved in getting estimates and supporting evidence to substantiate a claim may discourage people. Secondly, the air force maintains that sonic booms created by aircraft flying under its directives at altitudes above 30,000 feet will not damage:

1. Concrete driveways, walks, slab floors, patios, basements, retaining walls, and like items.
2. Concrete, block or stone construction, brick or stone chimneys, brick or stone veneer, mortar joints, and like items.
3. Directly damage automobile glass, television safety screens, television picture

tubes, electronic components of television or radio sets, water closets and commodes, and like items.

If the air force denies that its aircraft was below 30,000 feet, for an individual claimant to prove otherwise is often impossible.

Operation of military aircraft at supersonic speeds over the United States has already resulted in widespread damage to national parks and wilderness areas. Between August 11 and December 22, 1966, some 83 sonic booms were recorded over Canyon de Chelly National Monument, Arizona. One of these booms loosened an estimated 80 tons of rock which fell on ancient Indian cliff dwellings causing irreparable damage. In testimony before a U.S. House Appropriations Committee that was released in May 1971, U.S. National Park Service Director George Hartzog, commenting on air force flights, said:

They blasted the face of canyons with sonic booms, destroyed prehistoric ruins at Yellowstone and Teton. There is never a quiet moment in either of those parks.

What is a 3,000 or 4,000 year old prehistoric ruin worth? What is the face of a cliff at Mesa Verde worth? It is shattered off and now is at the bottom of the canyon.

Even if the SST is initially operated at supersonic speeds only on overwater flights, it still poses two serious difficulties. B. Lundberg, of the Swedish Aeronautical Research Institute, has analyzed the available data on overwater operations in his excellent report, *Acceptable Nominal Sonic Boom Overpressure in SST Operation Over Land and Sea*. The greatest concentration of SST routes in the world would be over the North Atlantic between North America and Europe. Of course, this area also has one of the highest concentrations of ships of all types of any area in the world. An estimated 4,000 persons would, on the average, be subjected to the boom from each SST flight across the North Atlantic. Furthermore, persons under these routes must expect one to two booms per hour day and night.[11,12]

There also exists a common misconception that *overwater* means *transoceanic* but this is not exactly the case. In an article entitled, "Our SST and Its Economics," John M. Swihart, of the Boeing Company, shows projected SST routes by 1990 throughout the Mediterranean and Carribean, through Hudson Bay, across the Arctic Circle, and through the Gulf of St. Lawrence. On eastbound flights from Montreal or Quebec supersonic operation would commence in the St. Lawrence River about 250 miles east of Quebec (in the vicinity of Baie-Comeau) and the route would proceed through either the Strait of Bell Island, Nfd., or through Cabot Strait separating Nova Scotia from Newfoundland. Prior to canceling its options on four Concordes on June 30, 1972, Air Canada had considered a supersonic corridor across Canada from a point in the vicinity of Baie-Comeau to the coast of Labrador north of Goose Bay. On any of these routes, an appreciable land area would be subjected to booms.[13,14]

The other, and in some respects more serious difficulty, is that mounting economic pressure to expand the market for the plan may ultimately result in overland routes. The Boeing Company's John M. Swihart, in the article noted previously, calculated that if supersonic operations were restricted to overwater and transpolar routes, by 1990 the world SST fleet would consist of 543 planes. In a report issued in 1968 the U.S. Institute for Defense Analysis estimated the total world market for SSTs to be only 279 aircraft if supersonic travel is restricted to overwater flights. Despite the glowing claims of the Boeing Company, the FAA, and the British Aircraft Corp. of a 500 airplane market, it became abundantly clear during congressional debate in the spring of 1971 on funding the Boeing 2707-300 that no one really knows for sure if there *is* a market, much less what that market might be. On March 19, 1971, the day after the U.S. House of Representatives voted to discontinue funding the Boeing SST, the president of the Chase Manhattan Bank in New York said there is no foreseeable market for the SST and to expect private investors to invest any money in the project was inconceivable to him. Robert Sikes, president of Continental Airlines, testified before the U.S. House Appropriations Committee that the Concorde could not be used profitably on the Mainland-Hawaii route. In a confidential study, United Air Lines reportedly found that it would have to fly the Concorde in a completely first-class configuration, charge a 50 percent surcharge, and obtain a 60 percent average load factor in order to realize a reasonable return on its investment. United has since cancelled its options for six of the planes.

In November of 1970, the British Aircraft Corp. announced that the Concorde's expected seat-mile costs would be 36 percent higher than those of the Boeing 747. Airlines will therefore be obliged to add a 35-40 percent surcharge for travel on the Concorde. There seem to be two principal reasons for this. One is the escalating cost of SSTs relative to the B-747 (the estimated price of the Concorde has jumped from $16 million in 1966 to $26 million in 1971 to $37.5 million in 1972).[15] The other is its voracious appetite for fuel.

British Aircraft Corp. and Aerospatiale, the French firm, in the joint venture, have begun concentrating on selling the Concorde as a businessman's aircraft that would show a profit even with the surcharged fares. A combined traffic forecast by BOAC and Air France estimated traffic between Canada and Europe would justify four round trips weekly by the Concorde. However, Air Canada concluded that even with a fare yield close to today's first class level, it would have to fly 42 round trips weekly in order to justify a fleet of four Concordes. Air Canada cancelled its Concorde options on June 30, 1972. It is worth noting, here, that first class transatlantic fares are approximately 60-70 percent higher than basic coach fares, and most tourists are able to utilize an even lower excursion fare. For example, in 1971 the following fares were in effect for scheduled round-trip service on the New York-Paris route: first class, $826; peak period economy, $596; basic economy, $496; 17-28 day excursion, $353; 29-45 day excursion, $297.

In 1972, Aerospatiale was predicting a market for 260 Concordes by 1980, but even that figure may amount to wishful thinking. After Pan American and TWA dropped their options in January 1973, the Concorde manufacturers were left with firm orders for only fourteen planes—nine from BOAC and Air France, three from China, and two from Iran. Unfortunately, Air France and BOAC, both government-subsidized airlines, seem certain to purchase the nine aircraft which they have on order.[16]

Furthermore, the range of the Concorde is only about 3,600 miles compared to nearly 6,000 miles for the Boeing 747 and DC-8-62. Because of this range limitation, the Concorde will probably be unable to operate on a nonstop route between New York and Rome, and there are doubts about its ability to even cross the North Atlantic with a full load of passengers and adequate fuel reserves. For this reason, transatlantic traffic will be confined largely to the North Atlantic and many of the routes will pass close to, if not over, Nova Scotia and Newfoundland. The FAA has reportedly been considering giving the Concorde preferential landing rights at New York's Kennedy Airport so that the plane would not run out of fuel while stacked in the holding pattern—a proposal that offers further proof, if any were needed, that the FAA is not interested in protecting the public from aircraft noise.[2]

If economic pressures mount and there is no federal legislation prohibiting SST operations at supersonic speeds, the FAA or the Canadian Department of Transport may allow overland flights. In hearings before the U.S. House Appropriations Committee in 1967, then Transportation Secretary Alan Boyd offered the following reply to a question from Rep. William Minshall (R., Ohio):

For example, going out of Chicago to the West Coast, I think it will be entirely possible to operate a route over the Plains area and possibly across the Canadian border without discomfort or inconvenience to people on the ground.

John Swihart predicts that within three months after delivery of the first SST to the carriers, SSTs will be used on the New York-Fairbanks route across Canada.[13]

The Senate-passed version of the Noise Control Act of 1972 contained a provision which would have prohibited the operation of civil aircraft over U.S. territory at a speed greater than Mach 1 except for certain research purposes. Unfortunately, the House of Representatives refused to accept this provision, and it was deleted in conference committee. Since it now appears likely that at least a few Concordes will enter commercial service, adoption of such legislation is essential. There is no reason to believe the FAA will permanently prohibit supersonic flights by civil aircraft over U.S. territory, and once supersonic aircraft enter commercial service, there will be enormous pressures to expand the market by permitting overland flight.[17,18]

Supersonic flight over Canada is not presently prohibited by statute. Section 515 of the Canadian Air Regulations states:

515. (1) No aircraft shall be operated in such a negligent or reckless manner as to endanger or be likely to endanger the life or property of any person.

   (2) Subject to subsection (3), no person shall fly an aircraft in such a manner as to create a shock wave or sonic boom, the effect of which may imperil the safety of other aircraft, be injurious to persons or animals, or cause damage to property.

   (3) The Minister may make orders or directives with respect to the operation of aircraft in sonic or supersonic flight.

Under this provision of the Air Regulations, the Ministry of Transport issued an Air Navigation Order on October 4, 1972 (SOR/72-408) which states that no person may operate an aircraft in supersonic flight over Canada unless authorized to do so by the Minister of Transport. However, this is much the same as saying that supersonic flight by civil aircraft over the United States is prohibited unless authorized by the FAA. Furthermore, the wording of Section 515 of the Air Regulations is subject to rather broad interpretation, since what is "injurious to persons or animals" is not defined. If SST flights over Canada commence, the Canadian government will have to come to grips with this problem. Adoption of more precise language, along the lines of that contained in the U.S. Senate bill, before SST overflights begin would surely prove to be an extremely fruitful endeavor. Language in the present regulation is neither clear nor adequate to protect the public and will almost certainly result in innumerable court battles. A bill (C-106) introduced in the House of Commons in February 1972 by Paul St. Pierre would have closed Canadian airspace to commercial SSTs. Unfortunately, it was never adopted.

The other aspect of the SST noise problem namely jet noise generated by the engines, has not received the publicity that has attended the sonic boom. Figure 6-17 shows the 100 PNdB noise contour for the Boeing 2707-300. Comparison of this contour with Figure 6-5, which shows noise contours for subsonic jets, reveals substantial differences in the noise characteristics between the SST and subsonic jets. These differences arise principally from the fact that the SST exhibits a much higher noise level at a given distance from the airplane but climbs out more steeply so that at a specified distance from the start of take-off roll it has attained a higher altitude than a subsonic jet. The net result is that the SST will produce much higher noise levels in the vicinity of airports, but beyond about four miles from the start of take-off roll, the noise level beneath the flight path will be somewhat less than for a subsonic jet such as the 707-320B. Note, however, that the noise radiation to the side of the runway during take-off is very much greater for the SST. Indeed, at a lateral distance of 2,130 feet (FAR Part 36 measuring point), the anticipated sideline noise level for the 2707-300 is 121 PNdB compared to about 111 for the 707-320B and about 102 for the B-747. Noise characteristics of the Concorde are similar to those of the Boeing 2707-300, though the levels appear to be somewhat lower. Recent figures from

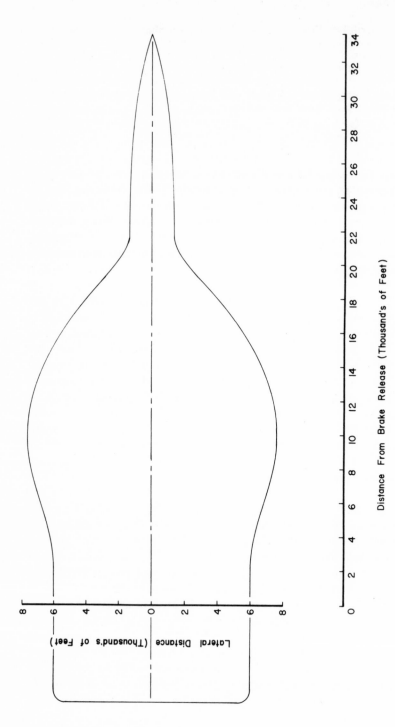

Distance From Brake Release (Thousand's of Feet)

Lateral Distance (Thousand's of Feet)

Figure 6-17. The 100 PNdB Noise Contour for the Boeing 2707-300 SST on Take-Off at Maximum Weight. Note: Area within this contour is approximately 12.5 square miles.[13]

Aerospatiale indicate a sideline noise level of about 114 PNdB. Data on the TU-144 are not available, but observers at the Paris air show in June 1971 reported very high take-off noise levels.

During all of the debate over the SST program in the U.S. Congress, a public need for such an airplane was never demonstrated, and a good many airline executives, privately at least, wish the SST would go away. British and Russian aircraft officials are counting on the so-called "Judas goat" theory, which holds that airlines must purchase any new equipment that embodies a real technological innovation, even if it operates at a loss, to avoid losing customers to competitors. The defeat of the Boeing SST prototype program in the U.S. Senate suggests that the traditional U.S. infatuation with technology may be coming to an end. Unfortunately, that act alone may not be sufficient to spare the world a new onslaught of noise. Governments will have to decide very soon whether they are going to bow to the irrationality of the "Judas goat" argument or preserve a world with some degree of sanity for their peoples. A compromise on this fundamental issue does not seem possible.

References

References

Chapter 1

1. Bridenbaugh, CITIES IN REVOLT, 24 (1964); quoted by G.A. Spater, "Noise and the Law," MICHIGAN LAW REVIEW 63, 1373-1410 (June, 1965).

2. A. Seidenbaum, Los Angeles TIMES (1967); quoted by W. Bronson, "Ear Pollution," CRY CALIFORNIA 2, No. 4, p. 28 (Fall, 1967).

3. L. Beranek, "The Effects of Noise on Man and Criteria for Its Control," PROCEEDINGS OF A SYMPOSIUM, ATMOSPHERIC NOISE POLLUTION AND MEASURES FOR ITS CONTROL, Univ. of California, Berkeley, June 17-21, 1968.

4. O. Schenker-Sprungli, "Down with Decibels," UNESCO COURIER (July, 1967).

5. TECHNOLOGY: PROCESSES OF ASSESSMENT AND CHOICE, Report of the National Academy of Sciences to the Committee on Science and Astronautics, U.S. House of Representatives, Washington, D.C. (July, 1969).

Chapter 2

1. A. Peterson and E. Gross, Jr., HANDBOOK OF NOISE MEASUREMENT (West Concord, Mass.: General Radio Co., 1967).

2. W. Rudmore, "Primer on Methods and Scales of Noise Measurements," PROCEEDINGS OF A CONFERENCE, NOISE AS A PUBLIC HEALTH HAZARD (Washington, D.C.: American Speech and Hearing Assn., February 1969).

3. C.M. Harris (ed.) HANDBOOK OF NOISE CONTROL (New York: McGraw-Hill, 1957).

4. L. Beranek, "Noise," SCIENTIFIC AMERICAN (Dec. 1966), pp. 66-76.

5. D.H. Eldredge, "Noise Induced Hearing Loss—Pathological Effects," paper presented at the AMA Sixth Congress on Environmental Health, Chicago, Illinois (April 28-29, 1969). Papers can be obtained from the American Medical Assn., 535 N. Dearborn Street, Chicago, Ill. 60610.

6. R. Gallo and A. Glorig, "Permanent Threshold Shift Changes Produced by Noise Exposure and Aging," AM. IND. HYGIENE ASSN. J. 25, 237 (1964).

7. A Cohen, J. Anticaglia, H. Jones, "Noise Induced Hearing Loss—Exposures to Steady State Noise," paper presented at AMA Congress on Environmental Health, Chicago, Ill. (April 28-29, 1969). (See reference 5)

8. "Safety and Health Regulations for Construction," FEDERAL REGISTER 36, Part II, No. 75 (April 17, 1971).

9. A. Glorig and J. Nixon, "Hearing Loss As a Function of Age," *Laryngoscope* 72, 1596 (November, 1962).

10. J. Dougherty and O. Welsh, "Community Noise and Hearing Loss," NEW ENG. J. MED. 275, 759 (October 6, 1966).

11. J. Lukas, "The Effects of Simulated Sonic Booms and Jet Flyover Noise on Human Sleep," paper presented at the AMA Congress on Environmental Health, Chicago, Ill. (April 28-29, 1969). (See reference 5)

12. G. Jansen, "Effects of Noise on Physiological State," PROCEEDINGS OF A CONFERENCE, NOISE AS A PUBLIC HEALTH HAZARD (Washington, D.C.: American Speech and Hearing Assn., February 1969).

13. W.H. Stewart, Keynote Address, PROCEEDINGS OF A CONFERENCE, NOISE AS A PUBLIC HEALTH HAZARD (Washington, D.C.: American Speech and Hearing Assn., February, 1969).

14. TOWARD A QUIETER CITY, Report of the New York Mayor's Task Force on Noise Control, New York Board of Trade (1970).

15. Noise Control Act of 1972, CONGRESSIONAL RECORD 118, S 18638 (October 18, 1972).

16. ENVIRONMENTAL NOISE CONTROL ACT OF 1972, Report of the Committee on Public Works, U.S. Senate on S.3342, Report No. 92-1160 (September 19, 1972).

17. Public Law 92-574, 86 Stat. 1234.

Chapter 3

1. L. Beranek, "The Effects of Noise on Man and Criteria for Its Control," PROCEEDINGS OF A SYMPOSIUM, ATMOSPHERIC NOISE POLLUTION AND MEASURES FOR ITS CONTROL, Univ. of California, Berkeley, June 17-21, 1968.

2. R. Berendt, G. Winzer, and C. Burroughs, A GUIDE TO AIRBORNE, IMPACT, AND STRUCTURE BORNE NOISE CONTROL IN MULTIFAMILY DWELLINGS, FT/TS-24 Federal Housing Admin., U.S. Dept. of Housing and Urban Development (Jan., 1968).

3. A. Peterson and E. Gross, Jr., HANDBOOK OF NOISE MEASURE-MENT (West Concord, Mass.: General Radio Co., 1967).

4. TENTATIVE RECOMMENDED PRACTICE FOR LABORATORY MEASUREMENT OF AIRBORNE SOUND TRANSMISSION LOSS OF BUILD-ING PARTITIONS, ASTM E90-66T, American Society for Testing and Materials, 1916 Race Street, Philadelphia, Pa.

5. SOLUTIONS TO NOISE CONTROL PROBLEMS IN APARTMENTS, MOTELS, AND HOTELS (Toledo, Ohio: Owens-Corning Fiberglas Corp., Fiberglas Tower).

6. FIELD AND LABORATORY MEASUREMENTS OF AIRBORNE AND IMPACT SOUND TRANSMISSION, ISO Recommendation R140-1960 (E), International Organization for Standardization (Jan., 1960).

147

7. MINIMUM PROPERTY STANDARDS FOR MULTIFAMILY HOUS-
ING, FHA No. 2600, Federal Housing Admin., U.S. Dept. of Housing and Urban
Dev. (June, 1969).

8. MINIMUM PROPERTY STANDARDS FOR ONE AND TWO LIVING
UNITS, FHA No. 300, Federal Housing Administration, U.S. Dept. of Housing
and Urban Development (November, 1966).

9. Noise Control Act of 1972, CONGRESSIONAL RECORD 118, S18638
(October 18, 1972).

10. TOWARD A QUIETER CITY, Report of the New York Mayor's Task
Force on Noise Control, New York Board of Trade (1970).

11. NATIONAL BUILDING CODE OF CANADA, 1970, prepared by the
Associate Committee on the National Building Code, National Research Council
of Canada, NRC No. 11246, Ottawa, Canada (1970).

Chapter 5

1. R. Donley, "Community Noise—What Is It and How Do We Measure It,"
PROCEEDINGS OF A SYMPOSIUM, ATMOSPHERIC NOISE POLLUTION
AND MEASURES FOR ITS CONTROL, Univ. of California, Berkeley, June
17-21, 1968.

2. E.P. Wilson, Chairman, Committee on the Problem of Noise, NOISE,
FINAL REPORT (London: Her Majesty's Stationery Office, 1963).

3. T. Mochizuki and N. Imaizumi, "City Noises in Tokyo," J. ACOUS.
SOC. JAPAN 23, 146-167 (1967).

4. W. Soroka, "Community Noise Surveys," PROCEEDINGS OF A CON-
FERENCE, NOISE AS A PUBLIC HEALTH HAZARD, (Washington, D.C.: Am.
Speech and Hear. Assn., February, 1969). Report may be obtained from the
American Speech and Hearing Assn., 9030 Old Georgetown Rd., Washington,
D.C. 20014.

5. TOWARD A QUIETER CITY, Report of the New York Mayor's Task
Force on Noise Control, New York Board of Trade, New York, N.Y. (1970).

6. USE OF MOTOR VEHICLE NOISE MEASURING INSTRUMENTS,
report of the California Highway Patrol to the California State Legislature (Jan.
1965).

7. "Urban Noise Control," COLUMBIA JOUR. OF LAW AND SOC.
PROBLEMS 4, 105-119 (March, 1968); reprinted in NOISE POLLUTION AND
THE LAW, J.L. Hildebrand (ed.) (Buffalo, N.Y.: Wm. S. Hein & Co., 1970).

8. PASSENGER CAR NOISE SURVEY, California Highway Patrol (January 1970). This report can be obtained from the California Highway Patrol, P.O.
Box 898, Sacramento, California 95804.

9. G.B. Craig, "California Laws and Regulations Relating to Motor Vehicle
Noise," presentation by the California Highway Patrol before the U.S. Environmental Protection Agency, San Francisco (September 28, 1971).

10. ENVIRONMENTAL NOISE CONTROL ACT OF 1972, Report of the Committee on Public Works, U.S. Senate on S.3342 (September 19, 1972).

11. L. Bourget and J.L. Beaton, CAN NOISE RADIATION FROM HIGHWAYS BE REDUCED BY DESIGN?, California Division of Highways, Materials and Research Dept., Rept. No. M & R 636316-1 (1968).

12. T. Priede, "Noise and Vibration Problems in Commercial Vehicles," J. SOUND AND VIBRATION 5, 129-154 (1967).

13. A.E.W. Austen and T. Priede, "Noise of Automotive Diesel Engines, Its Causes and Reduction," S.A.E. Preprint 1000A (1965).

14. T. Priede, "Origins of Noise of Various Automotive Prime Movers and Vehicles," PROCEEDINGS OF A SYMPOSIUM, ATMOSPHERIC NOISE POLLUTION AND MEASURES FOR ITS CONTROL, Univ. of California, Berkeley, June 17-21, 1968.

15. F. Juhasz, "Noise Reduction by Acoustic Enclosures for Internal Combustion Engines," M.T.Z. 29, No. 1, pp. 11-14 (1968).

16. T. Priede, A.E.W. Austen, and E.C. Grover, "Effect of Engine Structure on Noise of Diesel Engines," proceedings of INST. OF MECH. ENGIN. 179, part 2A, No. 4 (1964-65).

17. "Motor Vehicle Safety Regulations," SOR/70-487, CANADA GAZETTE PART II, 104, No. 22 (January 25, 1970).

Chapter 6

General Aircraft Noise

1. A. Peterson and E.E. Gross, Jr., HANDBOOK OF NOISE MEASUREMENT (West Concord, Mass.: General Radio Co., 1967).

2. W.C. Sperry, AIRCRAFT NOISE EVALUATION, FAA Rept. No. 68-34 (September, 1968), Office of Noise Abatement, Federal Aviation Administration, U.S. Dept. of Transportation, Washington, D.C.

3. Noise Standards; Aircraft Type Certification, Part 36, Volume III, Federal Aviation Regulations, Federal Aviation Administration, U.S. Dept. of Transportation, Washington, D.C. 20590.

4. AIRCRAFT NOISE, Annex 16 to the Convention on International Civil Aviation, International Standards and Recommended Practices, International Civil Aviation Organization, Montreal (August 1971).

5. AMERICAN AIRLINES, INC. V. TOWN OF HEMPSTEAD, 272F Supp. 226 (1966).

6. U.S. LAW WEEK 37, 3247 (1969).

7. Lyman Tondel, Jr., "Noise Litigation at Public Airports," ALLEVIATION OF JET AIRCRAFT NOISE NEAR AIRPORTS, Report of the Jet Aircraft Noise Panel, U.S. Office of Science and Technology, Washington, D.C. (March, 1966).

8. Herbert Tenzer, "Jet Aircraft Noise: Problems and Their Solutions," NEW YORK LAW FORUM 13, 465-75 (Summer, 1967).

9. UNITED STATES V. CAUSBY, 328 U.S. 256 (1946).

10. James D. Hill, "Liability for Aircraft Noise; The Aftermath of CAUSBY and GRIGGS," UNIVERSITY OF MIAMI LAW REVIEW, 19, 1-32 (Fall, 1964); reprinted in NOISE POLLUTION AND THE LAW, J.L. Hildebrand (ed.) (Buffalo, New York: Wm. S. Hein & Co., 1970).

11. See GRIGGS V. ALLEGHENY COUNTY, U.S. 369, 84 (1962).

12. See BATTEN V. UNITED STATES 306F, 2d 580 (10th cir., 1962), cert. den., 371 U.S. 955 (1962).

13. "Jet Noise in Airport Areas," MINNESOTA LAW REVIEW 51, 1087-1117 (June, 1967); reprinted in NOISE POLLUTION AND THE LAW (Ref. 10).

14. J.O. Powers, AIRBORNE TRANSPORTATION NOISE, ITS ORIGINS AND ABATEMENT (Washington, D.C.: Office of Noise Abatement, Federal Aviation Administration, U.S. Dept. of Transportation).

15. W.C. Sperry, J.O. Powers, S.K. Oleson, THE FEDERAL AVIATION ADMINISTRATION AIRCRAFT NOISE ABATEMENT PROGRAM, Office of Noise Abatement, FAA, U.S. Dept. of Transportation. Paper prepared for the International Gas Turbine Conference, Am. Soc. Mech. Engin., Washington, D.C., March 17-21, 1968.

16. J.B. Large and R.A. Mangiarotty, SOME ASPECTS OF THE DEVELOP-MENT OF QUIETER AIRCRAFT (Seattle, Wash.: The Boeing Co., November 1966), paper presented at the International Conference on the Reduction of Noise and Disturbance Caused by Civil Aircraft, London, England, November 22-30, 1966.

17. L.L. Beranek, "General Aircraft Noise," PROCEEDINGS OF A CON-FERENCE, NOISE AS A PUBLIC HEALTH HAZARD, Washington, D.C. (February, 1969); available from the American Speech and Hearing Assn., 9030 Old Georgetown Rd., Washington, D.C.

18. ALLEVIATION OF JET AIRCRAFT NOISE NEAR AIRPORTS, Report of the Jet Aircraft Noise Panel, U.S. Office of Science and Technology, Washington, D.C. (March, 1966).

19. Bolt, Beranek, and Newman, Inc., NOISE FROM AIRCRAFT USING VARIOUS DEPARTURE PROCEDURES AT LOS ANGELES INTER-NATIONAL AIRPORT, A Report to the Los Angeles Dept. of Airports (May, 1970).

20. E.P. Wilson, Chairman, Committee on the Problem of Noise, NOISE, FINAL REPORT (London: Her Majesty's Stationery Office, July 1963).

21. K.D. Kryter, "Evaluation of Psychological Reactions of People to Aircraft Noise," ALLEVIATION OF JET AIRCRAFT NOISE NEAR AIR-PORTS (Ref. 7).

22. TOWARD A QUIETER CITY, Report of the New York Mayor's Task Force on Noise Control, N.H. Anderson, chairman, New York Board of Trade (1970).

23. S. Goldstein, "Legal and Practical Limitations on Noise Control Methods," Report, Committee No. 4, INTERNATIONAL CONFERENCE ON THE REDUCTION OF NOISE AND DISTURBANCE CAUSED BY CIVIL AIRCRAFT, London (November, 1966). For a more extensive treatment of this subject, see also S. Goldstein, "A Problem in Federalism, Property Rights in Air Space and Technology," ALLEVIATION OF JET AIRCRAFT NOISE NEAR AIRPORTS, Report of the President's Jet Aircraft Noise Panel, Office of Science and Technology, Executive Office of the President (March, 1966).

24. J.E. Stephen, Statement, Hearings before the Committee on Interstate and Foreign Commerce, U.S. House of Representatives, Washington, D.C. (March, 1967). See also "Aircraft Noise," ENVIRONMENTAL SCIENCE & TECH. 1, No. 12, 979 (December, 1967).

25. J.J. Kaufman, "Legal Aspects of Noise Control," CONGRESSIONAL RECORD 115, E9031 (October 29, 1969).

26. Oscar Bakke, "Air Traffic Control and Flight Procedures," ALLEVIATION OF JET AIRCRAFT NOISE NEAR AIRPORTS (Ref. 7).

27. WASHINGTON NATIONAL AND DULLES INTERNATIONAL AIRPORT FORECASTS, FISCAL YEARS 1970-1981, Office of Aviation Economics, Federal Aviation Admin., U.S. Dept. of Transportation (November, 1969).

28. "Part 36—Noise Standards: Aircraft Type Certification," FEDERAL REGISTER 34, 18355 (November 18, 1969).

29. M.L. Yaffee, "Economics of Noise Rules Studied," AVIATION WEEK & SPACE TECH. 94, 40 (April 12, 1971).

30. J.D. Reilly, Statement NOISE POLLUTION, Hearings before the Subcommittee on Air and Water Pollution, U.S. Senate Public Works Committee on S. 1016, S. 3342, and H.R. 11021, March 24, 1972 in San Francisco and April 12 and 13, 1972 in Washington, D.C. (1972).

31. FEDERAL REGISTER 34, 453 (January 11, 1969).

32. ECONOMIC IMPACT OF IMPLEMENTING ACOUSTICALLY TREATED NACELLE AND DUCT CONFIGURATIONS APPLICABLE TO LOW BY-PASS TURBOFAN ENGINES, FAA Rept. 70-11, Rohr Corp., Chula Vista, California (July, 1970).

33. M.R. Segal, AIRCRAFT NOISE: THE RETROFITTING APPROACH, Congressional Research Service Rept. 72-78SP, HE9901 (March 1972).

34. HANDBOOK OF AIRLINE STATISTICS (Washington, D.C.: Bur. of Accounts & Statistics, U.S. Civil Aeronautics Board, 1972).

35. James K. Carr, Statement, NOISE POLLUTION, Hearings before the Subcommittee on Air and Water Pollution. (See Ref. 30.)

36. J. Donald Reilly, Communication to Sen. John Tunney, September 14, 1972, ENVIRONMENTAL NOISE CONTROL ACT OF 1972, Report of the Committee on Public Works, U.S. Senate to accompany S.3342 (September 19, 1972).

37. George Spater, American Airlines, Communication to Sen. John Tunney, September 15, 1972, ENVIRONMENTAL NOISE CONTROL ACT OF 1972, Report of the Committee on Public Works, U.S. Senate to accompany S.3342 (September 19, 1972).

38. AVIATION IN CANADA, 1971, a Statistical Handbook of Canadian Civil Aviation, Statistics Canada, Ottawa (February 1972).

39. FAA AIR TRAFFIC ACTIVITY, CALENDAR YEAR 1971, Federal Aviation Admin., U.S. Dept. of Transportation (February 1972).

40. M.C. Branch and R.D. Beland, OUTDOOR NOISE AND THE METRO-POLITAN ENVIRONMENT; A CASE STUDY OF LOS ANGELES WITH SPECIAL REFERENCE TO AIRCRAFT, Los Angeles City Planning Dept. (1970).

41. AVIATION WEEK & SPACE TECH., p. 30 (February 25, 1972).

42. CANADA YEAR BOOK, 1969, Statistics Canada, Ottawa.

43. CANADA YEAR BOOK, 1970-71, Statistics Canada, Ottawa.

44. HANDBOOK OF AIRLINE STATISTICS, Bureau of Accounts and Statistics, U.S. Civil Aeronautics Board, Washington, D.C. (1969).

45. NORTHEAST CORRIDOR AIR TRAFFIC AND HIGH SPEED GROUND TRANSPORTATION, Office of Aviation Economics, Federal Aviation Admin., U.S. Dept. of Transportation (March, 1970).

46. RAIL PASSENGER STATISTICS IN THE NORTHEAST CORRIDOR, Office of High Speed Ground Transportation, U.S. Dept. of Transportation (September, 1969).

47. Edmund Muskie, "Minority Views of Mr. Muskie," ENVIRONMENTAL NOISE CONTROL ACT OF 1972, Report of the Committee on Public Works, U.S. Senate to accompany S.3342 (September 19, 1972).

Sonic Boom

1. CONGRESSIONAL RECORD 116, No. 193, S 19388 (December 3, 1970).

2. Albert R. Karr, "Die-Hard Supporters of Supersonic Airliner Plot to Revive Project," WALL STREET JOURNAL (November 1, 1972).

3. J.O. Powers and D.J. Maglieri, A SURVEY OF SONIC BOOM EXPERI-MENTS (Washington, D.C.: Office of Noise Abatement, Federal Aviation Administration, U.S. Dept. of Transportation).

4. C.W. Nixon, "Sonic Boom—A Community Study," PROCEEDINGS OF A CONFERENCE, NOISE AS A PUBLIC HEALTH HAZARD, Washington, D.C. (February, 1969). (See Ref. 17 under general aircraft noise.)

5. B. Lundberg, "Acceptable Nominal Sonic Boom Overpressure in SST Operation," PROCEEDINGS OF A CONFERENCE, NOISE AS A PUBLIC HEALTH HAZARD, Washington, D.C. (February, 1969). (See Ref. 4.)

6. W.F. Baxter, "The SST: From Watts to Harlem in Two Hours," STANFORD LAW REVIEW 21, 1-57 (Nov., 1968); Reprinted in NOISE POLLUTION AND THE LAW. (See Ref. 10 under general aircraft noise.)

7. D.L. Lansing and D.J. Maglieri, COMPARISON OF MEASURED AND CALCULATED SONIC BOOM GROUND PATTERNS DUE TO SEVERAL DIFFERENT AIRCRAFT MANEUVERS, NASA Tech. Note No. D-2730 (April 1965).

8. H.H. Hubbard, D.J. Maglieri, and D.A. Hilton, GROUND MEASURE-MENTS OF SONIC BOOM PRESSURES FOR THE ALTITUDE RANGE 10,000 to 75,000 FEET, NASA Tech. Rept. No. R-198 (July, 1964).

9. D.J. Maglieri, T.L. Parrott, D.A. Hilton, and W.L. Copeland, LATERAL SPREAD SONIC BOOM GROUND PRESSURE MEASUREMENTS FROM AIRCRAFT AT ALTITUDES TO 75,000 FEET AND AT MACH NUMBERS TO 2.0, NASA Tech. Note No. D-2021 (November, 1963).

10. W. McCormack, "Damage Experience," Proceedings of ASHA Conf. (Ref. 4.)

11. B. Lundberg, ACCEPTABLE NOMINAL SONIC BOOM OVERPRES-SURE IN SST OPERATION OVER LAND AND SEA, L-14 (1968), Swedish Aeronautical Research Institute.

12. William A. Shurcliff, SST AND SONIC BOOM (New York: Ballantine Books, 1970).

13. J.M. Swihart, "Our SST and Its Economics," ASTRONAUTICS AND AERONAUTICS 8, 30-51 (April 1, 1970).

14. "Structure, Schedule Spur Concorde Verdict," AVIATION WEEK & SPACE TECH. 97, No. 10 (September 4, 1972).

15. Herbert Coleman, "Concorde Seen Profitable Despite Fare," AVIATION WEEK & SPACE TECH. 97, No. 20 (November 13, 1972).

16. "Concorde Outlook," AVIATION WEEK & SPACE TECH. 96, No. 11, p. 65 (March 13, 1972).

17. CONGRESSIONAL RECORD VOL. 118, S18639 (October 18, 1972).

18. NOISE POLLUTION, Hearings before the Subcommittee on Air and Water Pollution, U.S. Senate Public Works Committee on S. 1016, S. 3342, and H.R. 11021, March 24, 1972 in San Francisco and April 12 and 13, 1972 in Washington, D.C. (1972).

Index

A-Weighted Sound Levels: of airborne engine noise, 75–76; calculation from octave bands, 12, 14; of construction equipment, 16, 57–58; conversion to PNL, 83; correlations with other scales, 83; defined, 11–12; of exhaust noise, 75–76; limits for motor vehicles, 65–68; measurement of, 11–12; of motor vehicles 61; of motorcycles, 79; in New York City, 60; in Philadelphia, 60; reductions for motor vehicles, 76–77, 79–80; in rooms, 28; in Tokyo, 60–62; typical values, 13

Acceptable Nominal Sonic Boom Overpressure in SST Operation Over Land and Sea, 136

Acoustical Materials: in buildings, 29–38, 43–52; in engine enclosures, 76; in jet engines, 87, 90, 105

Acoustical terminology, 5–14

Aeronautics Act, 117

Air Canada, 100, 110, 111, 115, 118; Concorde options, 136, 137; supersonic route, 136; wide-bodied jets, 100

Air Commerce Act, 85

Air Line Pilots Association, 99

Air Services Branch, 117

Air traffic, *see* Aircraft; Air transportation

Air Transport Association, 96, 107

Air transportation: growth of, 110–111, 114–118; in northest corridor, 118–119, 122; regulation of, 116–118, 121–123; route structure, 116–118; statistics, 110–116, 118

Airborn sound isolation: determination of required, 35, 37–38; FHA criteria for, 41, 43–45; FHA requirements for, 43–44, 46; measurement of, 31; requirements in Germany, 49–51; single-figure ratings for, 35–38, 49–51; *see also* Sound Transmission Class; Sound transmission loss; sound isolation

Aircraft: approach profile, 91, 93; Canadian air carrier fleet, 100–101, 115; jet engines, 86–90; operations, 110–115, 116; regulation of operations, 96–99, 117–118, 121–123, 138–139, 141; SST, *see* Supersonic transport; take-off flight profile, 90–91; traffic pattern at LAX, 91, 94; U.S. air carrier fleet, 106–109

Aircraft noise: abatement procedures, 97–99; characteristics of, 86–92; effects on dreaming, 24; effects on sleep, 22–24; lawsuits, 84, 95; legal aspects of, 84–86; legislative regulation of, 84–86, 96–97, 100, 121–123; rating scales for, 83–84; regulations, 95, 96–99, 121–123; sources of, 86–90; from SSTs, *see* Supersonic transport; standards, 100–104, 110; surveys, 94, 95, 115

Aircraft Noise Abatement Act, 100

Aircraft noise control: through alternate transportation, 118–122; through certification standards, 100–105, 110; coordinated approach to, 121–123; in jet engine design, 86–90; through legislation, 96–97, 100, 121–123; through nacelle modification, 105; through operating procedures, 97–99; through retrofitting, *see* Retrofitting; through traffic reduction, 116–119, 121–123

Aircraft Noise Evaluation, 84

Aircraft Noise: International Standards and Recommended Practices (Annex 16), 83–84, 110

Aircraft noise levels: and engine thrust, 86–91; for existing aircraft, 100, 102–103, 106; FAR Part 36, 101–103; landing, 91, 93–94; near LAX, 91, 93–94; for retrofitted aircraft, 105–107, for SSTs, 139–141; take-off, 90–92; tolerance of, 94

Airport Operators' Council International, 96, 103, 104, 109

Airports: land use planning near, 99; location of, 99–100, 115–116; regional, 115–116; *see also specific airports*

Alaska, 2, 138

Alaska Airlines, 2

Alberta, control of motor vehicle noise in, 63, 65, 70–71, 73

Allen, William, 124

Alleviation of Jet Aircraft Noise Near Airports, 99

Ambient noise, 8–9, 35, 37–38, 93, 97

American Society for Testing and Materials (ASTM), 31, 35, 49

Amplitude, 5–6, 9

Analyzers: defined, 12; octave band, 12; one-third octave band, 12, 14

Annoyance: of aircraft noise, 90–95, 115; considerations of, 23; rating scales for, 23, 83; of sonic booms, 130–134; *see also* Loudness

158

Reilly, J. Donald, 103, 104
Resolute Bay, 3
Retrofitting: advanced system, 107; cost
  estimates, 105–109; financing of, 110;
  noise reductions, 105–107
Rohr Corp. study, 105–109
Rosen, Dr. Samuel, 21
Royal Board of Civil Aviation, 123
Ryan, Rep. William, 19

St. Pierre, Paul, 139
San Bernardino mountains, 2
San Francisco, 83, 134
San Francisco International Airport: map
  of, 98; operations at, 97; preferential
  runway system, 97
Santa Barbara, 84
Saskatchewan, control of motor vehicle
  noise in, 63, 70–71
Seattle-Tacoma International Airport, 95
Seidenbaum, Art, 1
Shaffer, John, 126
Shock waves: dissipation of, 130; effects of
  aircraft maneuvers on, 130; generation
  of, 126–128; intensity 128–132;
  pressure signatures, 126–129, 131–132
Sierra Nevada, 2
Sikes, Robert, 137
Snowmobiles, see Motor vehicle noise;
  Motor vehicle noise codes;
  Motor vehicle noise control
Solutions to Noise Control Problems in
  Apartments, Motels, and Hotels, 33, 36,
  40, 42
Sonic boom, 124–139; carpet, 128, 131;
  damage, 134–136; duration of, 129,
  131–132; Edwards Air Force Base tests,
  129, 131–132; effects of aircraft
  maneuvers on, 130; effects on dreaming, 24; effects on sleep, 22–23; legislation, 138–139, 141; magnified intensities, 130; Oklahoma City tests, 130–
  134; production of, 127–128; regulation of, 138–139, 141; strength, 128–
  132; see also Shock waves
Sound: defined, 5; energy, 5, 9–10, 79, 86;
  frequency, see Frequency; pitch of, 5;
  point source of, 9–10; power, 7–8, 51;
  production of, 5, 7; speed of, 126;
  transmission in dwellings, see Dwellings;
  wave, 5–6, 9–10
Sound intensity: defined, 5; determination
  of, 7–9; threshold, 7; variation with
  distance, 9–10
Sound intensity level: calculation of, 7–10;
  defined, 7; how to combine, 7–9;
  loudness of, 9–11

Sound isolation: airborne, see Airborne
  sound isolation; in dwellings, 29–52;
  impact, see Impact noise isolation;
  measurement of airborne, 31;
  measurement of impact, 38–42
  requirements in building codes, 30;
  single-figure ratings for, 35–42
Sound level: A-weighted scale, 11–12, 14;
  how to combine, 7–9; measurement
  of, 11–12, 14; typical A-weighted, 13;
  variation with distance, 9–10; weighting networks for, 11–12, 14, 83;
  see also Noise level; Sound intensity
  level
Sound level meter, 5, 11–12, 14, 78–79, 83;
  precautions in use of, 78–79
Sound pressure level, 5, 12, 14; see also
  Sound level meter
Sound Transmission Class (STC): defined,
  35; determination of, 35–36; FHA criteria, 41, 43–45; FHA requirements,
  43–44, 46; National Building Code of
  Canada requirement, 47–48; New York
  City building code requirement, 46–47;
  use of, 35–38; of wall partitions, 32–34,
  35–38
Sound transmission loss: curves for wall
  partitions, 32–34, 36; defined, 31;
  determination of, 31; example of use of,
  35, 37–38
Speech: frequency range of, 27; intelligibility of, 27–28; masking of, 27–28
Speech Interference Level (SIL): defined,
  27; table of, 27; use of, 27–28
SST, see Supersonic transport
Standard "tapping machine", 38–39, 41, 51
Stephen, John E., 96
Stockholm, 123
Strategic Air Command, 134
Supersonic transport (SST), 3, 124–141;
  appropriations for 124, 126; Boeing,
  124–126, 136–137, 139–140;
  Concorde, 124–126, 131–132, 136–139,
  141; cost, 124–126, 137; data on 125,
  130–131, 136–141; engine noise, 126,
  139–141; environmental consequences
  of, 126; legislation, 138–139, 141;
  market for, 137–138; regulation of,
  138–139; routes across Canada, 136,
  138; sonic boom from, see Sonic boom;
  Shock waves; TU-144, 124–125, 141
Sweden, 51, 95, 123
Swihart, John M., 136, 137, 138
Switzerland, 95

Technology: Process of Assessment and
  Choice, 2

About the Author

Donald F. Anthrop, Associate Professor of Environmental Studies at California State University, San Jose, is a scientist who specializes in environmental problem-solving. He holds the B.S. degree in chemistry from Purdue University and the Ph.D. in materials science from the University of California at Berkeley. Professor Anthrop has lectured extensively on noise pollution and is the author of widely-quoted journal articles on the subject which were published in *Bulletin of Atomic Scientists* and the University of Toronto *Law Journal*.